I0009774

Kubernetes

The ultimate beginners guide to effectively learn Kubernetes step-by-step

Mark Reed

© Copyright 2019 - All rights reserved.

It is not legal to reproduce, duplicate, or transmit any part of this document in either electronic means or in printed format. Recording of this publication is strictly prohibited and any storage of this document is not allowed unless with written permission from the publisher except for the use of brief quotations in a book review.

Table of Contents

Introduction

The history of computer science can be characterized by the development of abstractions that aim at reducing complexity and empowering people to create more sophisticated applications. However, the development of scalable and reliable applications is still more challenging than it should be. To reduce the complexity, containers and container orchestration APIs such as Kubernetes have been introduced as crucial abstractions that radically simplify the development of scalable and reliable systems. Though orchestrators and containers are in the process of being absorbed into the mainstream, they do a great job at enabling the developers to create and deploy applications with agility, reliability, and, above all, speed.

Kubernetes has become the de-facto platform used for deploying and managing cloud native applications. Evidently, the adoption of Kubernetes has developed to be used in more complex and mission-critical applications. As such, enterprise operations teams ought to be conversant with Kubernetes to effectively manage any challenges that may arise. Note that developer experience, operator experience, and multi-tenancy are the core challenges that Kubernetes users encounter. Though the complexity of using and operating Kubernetes may be a huge concern, enterprises that manage to overcome the challenges enjoy different benefits, such as increased release frequencies, faster recovery from failures, quicker adoption of cloud technologies, and an improved customer experience that, in turn, offers a myriad of business advantages. The good news is that developers have the freedom to ensure faster innovations, while the operations teams ensure that resources are utilized efficiently and compliance is upheld.

This book focuses on explaining the management and design of Kubernetes clusters. As such, it covers in detail the capabilities and services that are provided by Kubernetes for both developers and daily users. The following chapters will take the reader through the deployment and application of Kubernetes, while taking into consideration the different user cases and environments. The reader will then gain extensive knowledge about how Kubernetes is organized, when it is best to apply various resources, and how clusters can be implemented and configured effectively. In the following chapters, you will gain an in-depth understanding of the Kubernetes architecture, the clusters, and how they are installed, how they operate, and how the software can be deployed through applying the best practices possible.

If you are new to Kubernetes, this book offers in-depth information that helps in understanding Kubernetes, its benefits, and why you need it. For instance, the following chapters give a detailed introduction to Kubernetes, containers, and development of containerized applications. It will further describe the Kubernetes cluster orchestrator and how tools and APIs are used to improve the delivery, development, and maintenance of distributed applications. You will understand how to move container applications into production by applying the best practices, and you will also learn how Kubernetes fits into your daily operations, ensuring that you prepare for production-ready container application stacks. This book aims at helping the reader comprehend the Kubernetes technology, along with educating on how to use the Kubernetes tooling efficiently and effectively, with the aim of developing and deploying apps to Kubernetes clusters.

Chapter One:
A Kubernetes Overview

What is Kubernetes?

Kubernetes is a Greek word used to define an open-source container orchestration system that is automated for deployment, scaling, and management. The first version of Kubernetes was released in July 2015 as a collaboration between Google and the Cloud Native Computing Foundation (CNCF). It makes it easier for a developer to package an application with the various elements it needs and finally come out as one package. For developers wanting to create more complex applications that require various elements involving multiple containers and machines, Kubernetes is an ideal solution. It can help application elements to restart and move across various systems as they are required to. It serves as the basic framework that allows users to choose the different frameworks, instruments, and the language, among other tools they may prefer. Even though Kubernetes is not a platform service tool, they still form a good basis for the development of these applications. Kubernetes is designed to help solve and offer modern application infrastructure solutions.

Its main unit of organization is called a **pod**. A pod is a group of containers that are taken as a group on a machine, and has the ability to communicate with one another easily. Each pod has a unique IP address, thereby ensuring that different applications can use similar ports without the risk of conflict. All containers using the ports can recognize each other as local hosts and can therefore correlate. These pods are organized into a service that works together to become a system of labels to store metadata in Kubernetes. These parts then create a systematic and consistent way to give predefined instructions via a command line center. A pod can define the volume of a network disk and relay the information to the containers in the pod. Pods are easily managed by setting up a control system, thus ensuring they are working properly.

Kubernetes does not limit the types of applications that are supported, and its main objective is to give support to a wide variety of workloads. It's important that people understand that Kubernetes does not give source codes, nor does it build the workload; instead, it determines the workflow of the application development and the technical requirements. Kubernetes does not do command logging, monitoring, or alerting solutions—it gives an integration to a mechanism that collects and exports metrics. It does not give any comprehensive configurations or management systems, which is left to the developer to ensure they create a good, self-healing system to protect their application. Kubernetes creates a no-need environment for orchestration and gives the user a continuous, current state that will eventually lead to the desired state. It makes it easier for users to move from the first step to the last step, thus avoiding the need to have an orchestration system. This makes Kubernetes an easy, efficient, powerful and resilient system. The ecosystem provided by Kubernetes ensures that there is a micro-based implementation to address the concerns of microservice. The efficiency of Kubernetes makes it the best in terms of information technology, and is widely used by many developers to ensure that their applications and software tools are efficient and flawless.

Kubernetes also has replica sets that ensure swift maintenance of the number of containers that have been assigned to one pod. A **selector**, in this case, is used to help the replica sets work properly; that is, it helps in good identification of the pods that are associated with every container. This sorts out what pods to add to which containers, and which to reduce or maintain. Kubernetes, being a multi-tier application, offers two modes of service discovery, beginning by first assigning stable IP addresses and DNS names to the services. These ensure that there is no traffic in the network and that the IP addresses match with those of the selector. In case of any defaults, the service is exposed inside or outside the cluster, depending on the load of traffic in the cluster network. Ample storage is readily available in the Kubernetes containers, since every pod restart tends to clear data on these containers. This, therefore, gives the pod enough space to serve them for a lifetime, even though this space can still be shared with other pods. The pod configuration determines the location at which every volume is mounted. Different containers can then mount their volume at different locations in the cluster network.

Kubernetes uses namespaces to ensure that there is a way of partitioning how various users apply the provisions given by Kubernetes. These namespaces can differentiate between development, production, and testing for various users, and they ensure there is a free environment for each Kubernetes user. ConfigMaps and Secrets in Kubernetes are used to help with changes in the configuration settings, which is to ensure that users find a better place to store and manage the information on these containers. Kubernetes store their memory in nodes that are used by the ConfigMaps and Secrets. If the information in these pods is deleted, then the information on the whole memory copy system in the ConfigMaps and Secrets is deleted as well. Users will only be able to access these pods through environment variables or in the container file system, which can only be accessed from within the pods—nowhere else in the system. Developers now have an easier time in the configuration and deployment of these applications. The advanced configuration of Kubernetes will ensure more efficient data protection and configuration. Kubernetes provides a good platform for cloud-native applications that require scaling and real-time data streaming, which is why most people see Kubernetes as an efficient and important tool in their work.

Why People Need Kubernetes

Developers look for good methods they can use package and run their applications, thereby ensuring fewer downtimes. Kubernetes saves the day by ensuring that your system is up and running all the time. It offers good value for people who use them, and many who have used it found it to be beneficial.

1. *Reproducibility*

Kubernetes ensures that if, for example, you delete the complete production environment you had before, you can recreate the same environment by using the backup data. Kubernetes helps you during disaster recovery, thus ensuring that you do not need to start the configuration all over again. This can only be achieved if you follow the instructions given by cloud providers. You can change your account and still be able to recover the data you had backed up. The concept of reproducibility brought out by Kubernetes helps you create a cloud account. If you use Terraform and Ansible to code everything for your

11

application, then the cost of your development might be higher than you thought it would. In the past, people spent time and money writing and generating codes for the configuration, but with the rise of Kubernetes, this is now as easy as a snap of a finger. With Kubernetes, you can easily describe everything in YAML (or YAML Ain't Markup Language) files. It also manages the DNS records that are required to bring together services. It gives you a chance to create a series of multiple infrastructures rather than having just one. You can also create a new setup demo by using YAML files and deploy them into different namespaces on the cluster system. To achieve this, users should be able to follow the right steps and do things the right way. Creating these containers ensures that you built them in a way that allows you to easily change the configuration settings. Always expect to have various or separate environments as you create your YAML files. The Continuous Integration (CI) system used should be able to create an easy environment, which is why the deployment process should be well-integrated. Kubernetes makes it easy for you and others who use it to achieve the desired results.

2. *Immutability*

Kubernetes has a special way of immutability, in that you do not have to update anything; rather, you would replace it. Traditionally, people used to upgrade their software every time there was a new or better version. Going through the hassle of upgrading to the software is over with the introduction of Kubernetes. If problems occurred while people updated their software, developers could experience a tough time looking for ways to fix the problem, and the hassle of reading through documents, troubleshooting, and looking for solutions online could be stressful. Kubernetes came up with a better way to cover the downtime needed when upgrading and updating— instead of updating your server, you would install a new server.

Before installing the new server, you would first need to ensure that it works perfectly and that it is compatible. If everything is okay with the new server, you can then go ahead and install it. A spare server is also essential, as it will be handy when it comes time to deploy the infrastructure. While undertaking these upgrades, you can also make sure that you have the virtual machines and cloud providers to make the work a bit easier. Manual installation or updates of servers can be time-consuming, which is why you need automated tools to continue with the installation.

Kubernetes ensures that it is easier for you to install the servers, as the concept and virtual machines used to set them up have been simplified. The person using Kubernetes will realize that the containers running on top of Kubernetes are secure if the correct installation methods are used, and the containers are replaced rather than adjusted. Kubernetes has made it possible for users, if there is a problem with the newer version, to easily switch back to the previous version. However, during this upgrade, you need to recognize that you do not need to change to the previous container after an upgrade. For example, if the new container version is not compatible with your previous database, the rejoining of the previous nodes can be difficult, and you may not be able to go back to the previous version of the database format if it has already been adjusted.

3. *Easier deployment*

The deployment on servers, at times, has been a tricky situation to handle. Before the release of Kubernetes, users needed to create a new version of the application on a different service directory, then switch the symlink to all the other servers. People would need to use empty caches and make sure to populate the database, so they could deploy the servers. When the containers were created, this process was simplified because the initialization of the containers was taken care of by the launching of the container. After the natural replacement of the containers, the caches would normally purge themselves. Kubernetes ensured that their system was well-protected, so there would be no containers launched that can damage the Kubernetes cluster.

Faster and easier deployment ensures that you also get a faster time to the market. The smaller breakdown of teams allows each team to focus on a set role and ensure that it is efficient. These teams can be specialized to support experts, who can then be assigned to support these multiple teams. This will help build your IT team, allowing it to handle large applications from as many containers as possible, as they have already been managing small teams.

Tinder is one application that has used Kubernetes to grow their journey into the market, and is known to be efficient and easy to use. Due to its high use, Tinder reported that they were struggling with scale and scalability. This is when they applied to outsource a reliable container system that could support them, and found Kubernetes to be their answer. Since then, their business operations have been smooth.

4. *Networking abstraction*

Writing an iptable script was one of the many traditional ways that people used to network. **Iptable** was a tool that had a lot of errors. Even after many attempts to fix it, there were still many things that could go wrong with the tool, and it became hard for developers to change it due to the knowledge they needed to have about it and the required permissions. The site admins would not let any requests for change to be handled by outsiders; therefore, only internal workers could take action and requests for change. However, Kubernetes networks and policies hide the complexity of their network and make the firewall rules easily deployable. They give clear instructions on how the application should be run by storing them in the **grit repository** (or grit repo). The other configuration settings for the application can also be found there. They can maintain their firewall, and they tend to use the Kubernetes audit tools to ensure security. This would be better rather than restricting firewall configurations that are used as compliance policies.

5. *Deploying and updating software at scale*

Deployment is a way to speed up the process used when building, testing, and releasing software. Most software does not support the deployment of these processes at scale, but Kubernetes does. Thanks to Kubernetes, you can maintain and change your application lifecycle. It has a deployment controller that can simplify complex tasks into easy ones; it can identify completed, in-process and failing deployments fast by balancing their capabilities; and it saves time, as it can easily pause a deployment and resume it later on. If the current or upgraded version is not stable, it can control the new version to revert to the earlier version. They have created more simplified deployment operations that include **horizontal auto-**

scaling, in which the scalar can measure the number of pods that can be depleted by a certain number of resources; **rolling updates** that give you the predefined number of limited pods and the spare pods that exist temporarily; and **canary deployments** that ensure that you simultaneously upgrade from the older version to the newer version.

6. Great for cloud multi-cloud adoption

Microservice infrastructure in these containers makes it easy for you to split your application into small components and run them in different environments and clouds. Kubernetes does not limit you and can be used anywhere—in public, private, or other hybrid clouds. This functionality enables you to reach out to users wherever they are, and makes it more secure. Many of today's businesses have grown to love and use this microservice, since it makes their tools more easily manageable.

7. IT Cost Optimization

If your company is operating on a massive scale, then Kubernetes has your budget covered. This is because it offers a container-based infrastructure that can package to different applications to help optimize how you use your cloud and hardware investments. Hardware and cloud management was a hard nut to crack for people who did not use Kubernetes, but since it's been developed, people are now enjoying using Kubernetes, as it caters for their budgets.

Spotify is one company that has benefitted cost-effectively from Kubernetes. According to Spotify, since they started using Kubernetes, they have been able to save their CPU utilization, thus leading to better IT optimization.

Importance of Kubernetes

1. *Portability*

Kubernetes offers an easy and faster way for deployment. Companies can benefit from using the available multiple clouds to grow their infrastructure even more. It does not tie you down to one system and its portability makes it even easier.

2. *Scalability*

This means that Kubernetes can be deployed anywhere, in all cloud environments. Their containers can run, even in bare metals or virtual machines. Due to recent changes and advancements in development and deployments, Kubernetes allows you to scale much faster than before. The orchestration system ensures that it improves the application performance automatically, which also helps optimize infrastructure utilization and makes it not just limited to the metrics, but also the resources used in the process.

A good example of a company that has been able to benefit from the scalability of Kubernetes is the LendingTree application. This application uses many microservices that act as a platform for their business operations. The horizontal scalability ensures that their clients can access the application, even when they are at their peak seasons. Kubernetes is responsible for ensuring that these applications are well-deployed and running all the time, and that the applications do not default.

3. *Highly available*

Kubernetes is available both at the application and infrastructure level. They also have a reliable storage system, therefore ensuring that there are readily available workloads. The configuration settings ensure that their multi-nodes replicate easily, thereby enhancing availability. Its availability makes it even better and more efficient to use, which is why developers and companies prefer it, as most other software does not allow for availability or replication. The success of the application you come up with does not depend on the features that it has, but on the availability of the application—if your application is unavailable or not working when you most need it, then you will be unable to make anything out of it.

This is why developers look forward to using Kubernetes, since it is always available and doesn't break down at crucial times. This is the best solution for companies that have had problems with their application unavailability.

4. *Open-source*

The open-source style gives developers the freedom to design work with Kubernetes, combined with the vast ecosystem that is available. It does not limit you to using the Kubernetes tools, but has ensured that the tools you choose to design your work with are compatible with the containers available. This open-source will help in the automation, deployment, scaling, and managing of your application, and you will also be able to run the application without having to waste time. The open-source feature also makes developers and companies want to use Kubernetes even more.

5. *Market leader without Competition*

People have a lot of trust in Google and Kubernetes, and the latter having been originally designed by Google means that this faith extends to the Google-designed system. It has instant credibility to people and has, therefore, ended up as the highest used application deployment system by developers. People have tried competing with Kubernetes, but have failed or not been able to match its reach.

Kubernetes can fix its security threats and does not have a lot of unnecessary traffic, since its system can clear this out from the network system. Due to this, it remains a leader in the market, with almost zero competitors.

Many developers have declared Kubernetes to be the next big thing over the next few years because they can see that the future in Kubernetes will continue to offer a set of wide infrastructure platforms for developers. Research has shown that students due to graduate over the next four or five years are keen to use Kubernetes for their application deployment. Being a virtualization admin means focusing on containers that can give you the best service, since virtualization is not only relevant to infrastructure teams, but developers as well. If you use the wrong containers for your application development, nobody will enjoy using the application you created. You might also end up being frustrated with the application and might even give it up, or end up spending more than you initially planned. This is why Kubernetes is known to be the best in terms of containers and application development, and the reason why it lacks competitors and will continue being the leader in the market

6. *While using Kubernetes, you can constantly monitor the performance of your deployment.*

It also gives you a good platform to keep a check on the different metrics regarding the components the system's design. It gives you the ability to showcase this easily and impactful.

7. *It gives you continuous integration and deployment that enables you to shift from one cloud to another during the production process.*

It does not limit you, and continuous integration will ensure that it keeps your deployment process up and running at all times. Developers do not like to work with a system that limits them to one integration and does not give them the chance to move from one suite to another during production. This feature enables developers to run their applications in real-time and without much hassle. The containers give you ample space and time for you to develop and process your application into the desired design.

8. *It gives you the ability to switch from one server to the other.*

Assume, for instance, that your company has five servers—two of the servers are overloaded and you want to reduce the load. The nodes available on these servers will give you the go-ahead as to which server to shift to, so you reduce the overload on these two servers. This is another important benefit of using Kubernetes: you do not have to put up with downtime due to the failure of one server and not being able to shift to the others. This is a reassuring feature of its use and a significant reason why developers value the system.

9. *It can run any containerized application.*

Kubernetes has been able to combine different strategies in ensuring that the tools required for you to build your application do not differ between applications. This is as cost-effective as when developers used to need different tools for each application process. As a result, a lot of people have been given a chance to build their future through Kubernetes. Existing applications can also run on Kubernetes, and it is easy for you to migrate the existing application from one server to the other.

A company should be keen, when sourcing for the best container system that can support their application development to the end, for this system to run efficiently. Kubernetes is one of those containers that a company would not want to miss out on, since it has all these desirable benefits. The cost-effectiveness, efficiency, and availability will give your company the best service applications that your customers will not regret using. The better and faster the application, the happier the users will be; the happier the users, the more users will use the application as a result. The more users and clients, the higher your business or company will grow. Developers now have an easy and efficient way of coming up with applications that will be of help to their clients, and clients are happy with efficient applications that do not keep on failing; therefore, companies that care about the concerns of their clients will use Kubernetes to ensure they fully satisfy their clients. In doing so, they also increase the company's sales and their popularity.

Chapter Two:
Kubernetes Architecture

Kubernetes, being the source platform that is normally essential for managing and deploying containers, creates a runtime and container-centric infrastructure necessary for application management. It also provides service delivery, a self-healing mechanism, and load-balancing across a variety of hosts. It can also be classified as an operating system that is much more superior to the container orchestrator for its cloud-native application, which is run just like in Windows, Linux, and MacOS.

The main aim of Kubernetes is to reduce the orchestrating burden when computing and networking, and in the storage infrastructure of the operating system. However developers usually focus on the operator's applications and container-centric workflow.

The main aim is usually to reduce the application burden and to enable container-centric workflow and self-service operation. In most cases, the developers can customize the workflow and create an automation that enables them to deploy and manage the application. This is done through multiple containers. The major workload, such as stateless applications monoliths and micro services, are used in application integration; however, Kubernetes is a flexible

25

platform that allows the consumer to exercise the functionalities à la carte, or by creating built-in functionality in the system. On the other hand, Kubernetes has additional capabilities based on the environment in which they work.

Therefore, a control plan that provides the system with the container records are all objects used in the application. It usually responds to the changes in the cluster, constantly managing the objects to match the desired object state.

The control plan is made up of major components such as Kube-controller-managers, Kube-API server, and live-scheduler. These are usually run on a single master node, or can be made available by the use of multiple master nodes.

Concepts

The API servers normally provide lifecycle orchestration, used for updates and scaling in different applications. They normally work as a gateway to the cluster, and they provide authentication platforms for clients by the use of the proxy or tunnel nodes. The servers always have some resources, such as metadata used for annotations, specifications, and observed states of data.

Most of the time, there are various controllers used to drive the state of the node's endpoint, replications that are also known as auto-scaling, and service accounts preferred as the namespaces in the system application. The controller manager runs the cool control loops, which are responsible for making changes in the drive status and watching the cluster status of the application system. It also drives statuses toward the desired state that is comprehensible to the users. On the other hand, the cloud controller manager takes the responsibility of integrating the public cloud toward optimal support in the available zones; for instance, the storage services and **virtual machine** (VM) system network services for DNS integrated for Cloud balancing.

The scheduler is usually used in the containers for scheduling across the nodes, usually taking various continents into account. Some limitations are encountered in the process, and there is no guarantee or affinity for the specifications used in the system.

Pods and Services

These are some of the crucial concepts of Kubernetes. They provide a platform through which the developers interact when integrating the system. The logical constructs are normally used for storage for data. Crucially, a single container is used alongside another container to run the configuration of the system.

On the other hand, vertically integrated application stacks are created by the use of the pods' form of WordPress application. These pods are represented as a running process of a cluster. It should be noted that pods are *ephemeral*, meaning they have a limited lifespan and should be used economically. This is because, when they are used during scaling upgrading of the system, they normally die in the process. Pods are best suitable for doing horizontal auto-scaling whereby they are enshrined in numbers. Therefore, they are good for doing the canary deployment and rolling updates.

There are various types of boards used in the system of Kubernetes. One such board is the replica set, which is relatively simple to be used with a limited number of pods run, thus making them the default use application. Secondly, there is a use of deployment, which creates a declarative pods manager via replica sets, including the rolling update mechanism and rollbacks. There is also a daemon set to create a node system used for log forwarding health monitoring, and the stateful set is integrated into the system for managing pods, maintaining the constant of the application.

Furthermore, services such as proxy configuration through a set of pods and IP address-based assignments are very important for the application. There are defined use pods creating a release of various new versions of applications, thus making the service easy-to-use. At any level, there are different requirements of the Kubernetes' use and assignment to different services, usually available inside the cluster through the use of IP services. These are only done using an internal access to the system, which is unavailable to outsiders, though different types allow external access such as load balancer type, commonly used for deployment. This type of balancer is usually used in the Cloud environment, which makes it more expensive and unavailable to many people. Apart from being expensive, it can also be perceived as complex for users.

The developers have come up with a simple way of solving the complexity and cost balance by integrating **ingress**, which is a high-level abstraction governing external access by the use of Kubernetes cluster hosts such as URL-based HTTP routing. However, there are many other different ingress controllers, such as ambassadors like Nginx, which support the cloud-native load balancer commonly used by Microsoft, Amazon, and Google. Interestingly, ingress is normally used in supporting multiple services under one IP address using the same load balancer. Beyond that, ingress is used for multiple other purposes such as configuration of resilience, simple routing rules authentication, and content-based routing.

Kubernetes has a distinct networking model, pod-to-pod and cluster-wide. There are various concepts used by Kubernetes to measure its volume capacity, which can be directories with data within that are made accessible to pods. However, there are many ways in which the directories are made available, and the contents are determined through a particular building type used in the system. Moreover, this content can be managed through a mixed pod, and most of the storage volume can be used up by the container pods. In most cases, the storage volume survives when the pods are restarted, or when they are deleted after the completion of work, depending on the storage type. However, with the block storage and mounting of pods, you don't need public cloud storage services, which can then be integrated into physical infrastructure storage like the fiber channel blocker known as iscsi, or GlusterFS. Some of the special accounts like ConfigMap and Secret are normally used in injecting information. These devices are used in Scratch space within the Kubernetes pods.

On the other hand, persistent volumes are generated into a storage resource by the administrator. There is a different kind of classified object that is linked to resources necessary for providing available consumption space. In every pod available in the system, Kubernetes sends a signal to the namespace normally made available; depending on the current usage of the PV, different states start making an annual invention and eliminate failures that may occur by not reclaiming the PV.

Ultimately, the abstraction layer underlying the storage compartment differentiating the quality is normally used by different characteristics, such as performance. Unlike the labels, the storage class operates depending on the task assigned to it at any level. The storage is dynamically provisioned based on the claims from pods, and pods are normally known for requesting storage space or expanding the space for new storage. Over time, the dynamic storage locations are used up by the public cloud providers.

Namespaces, usually referred to as the virtual cluster, are why multiple teams use virtual separated environments. These are necessary to prevent teams hindering each others' activities, thus not limiting them from external access. Labels are strategically used to distinguish resources. Within a single namespace, they normally have key attributes that describe or organize them to their subsets. In this case, labels are used to create efficient queries that are essential for user-oriented interfaces in the map allocation structures of Kubernetes objects.

Furthermore, labels are used to describe the state for testing and production or customer identification. Doctors tend to use the labels to filter or select objects

31

from hindering Kubernetes' hard links objects, and annotations are used arbitrarily as non-identifying matter or a declaration of configuration tooling. Image information from the people who are responsible for building the system is used up during annotations.

Kubernetes control plane is used as communication processing in the cluster. On the other hand, the control plane normally used as the record keeper of all the objects in the system run through continuous control loops and managed through various object states. The control planes tend to respond to changes in the cluster and make the object match the desired state, as directed by the developer. The Kubernetes control plane normally creates an instruction platform, in which the user can send applications and receive instruction scheduling through the cluster nodes to match the desired state.

Kubernetes Structure

The master node hosts tend to create services, which enable the administrator and orchestrate the Kubernetes control plane to set namespace, which then serve pods and the API server.

The Kubernetes structure uses **etcd**, which is an open-source that gives it room created within the CoreOS team. This key structure is normally managed by the Cloud Native Computing Foundation, which is responsible for distributing the UNIX directory. Here is where most of the global configuration file lives within the machines. It also provides a platform for the cluster server and the operating systems, which include the Linux OSX.

The etcd structure is fully replicated, whereby the entire system can create a cluster of nodes. It is also designed to create more space for hardware and network issues that may arise in the system. This structure is made in such a way that every read returns to the initial, intended purpose, which is consistent with a goal and objective of Kubernetes. Not to mention, the system is designed in such a way that all well-defined interfacing API is implemented with automatic TLS for authenticity. It is also marked with 10,000 writes per second, thus making it reliable and suitable for the use of Raft algorithms.

The etcd has a leader component that is reliable for cluster consensus, which is not primarily the request consensus, but the reads that can be processed by any member. Moreover, these leaders are responsible for replicating the information, accepting new changes, and responding to the nodes, thus committing after the receipts have been verified by the system. At any given point, clusters can only have one leader. In case the leader dies, the nodes are responsible for conducting a new election within a set time and when they must select a new leader. During that time, there is a rumble randomize election timer, which represents the amount of time the nodes maintained before conducting a new election for the intended candidate choice.

If, by any chance, there is no leader selected, the nodes are prone to restart a new term by marking themselves as the suitable candidate, and they seek votes from nodes. In this case, nodes are only responsible for voting for the first candidate who seeks their vote. So, if a candidate garnered more votes from the nodes cluster, it becomes the new leader, despite the potential bias in timing with which the candidate may have become leader irrespective of the votes garnered.

After electing their new leader, any change is directed to the leader nodes, but instead of accepting changes immediately, the etcd algorithm creates a platform where the majority vote matters in making the change. After the process has been done successfully, the new leader proposes cluster value to be used by the nodes, after which the receipts are confirmed. If the majority of nodes confirm the new value, the leader is supposed to commit the value to the log. For an order to be committed, there needs to be a quorum in the cluster nodes.

Docker Container

Critically, the Kubernetes automates the deployment and containerizes the application in a more manageable way, but they require base images that enable them to push to the Central container registry for the cluster nodes. Therefore, the **Docker hub** is essentially used to get the image for deployment and sharing to various interfaces. For these reasons, Dockers tend to be a very popular choice among developers of the Kubernetes system. The Dockers are technically made up of instructions and files installed in their system for reference purposes of the images. Also, there are executive configuration commands that create application dependency on the running container. To add, the Dockers have special images that are normally combined with the remote control services, like GitHub, to trigger the action. These can be in the form of Tooling or other automation services.

The development of Docker images and Hugo sites are personalized on the computer. In this case, users need to install Docker CE, Hugo, and a unique version control software like Git.

The Kubelet Cluster

Kubernetes are designed so they run in the background, where they are decoupled with the CLI tool. Since they are daemon, they tend to maintain an init system within themselves for the propagation of DEBS system configuration. The kublets are managed by the users of different services, though they are configured manually.

In most instances, configuration details of kubelets in the cluster are configured the same, while others are set as per the specifications. Different characteristics of the machines are accommodated within the network storage and machine OS. This configuration can be managed manually by the use of API type.

The configuration pattern of the kubelets is managed by the use of CRI runtime or other default subnet settings in the form of kubeadm join and kubeadm command. Users can manually integrate the instructions by passing them through a service-CIDR parameter. Through such subnets, virtual IPS are allocated to the DNS address through the use of a cluster DNS flag, though there is a need for making all the settings the same for every node in the cluster. In this application for a version structured API that configures every push made by the configurator cluster, the components that are responsible for such actions is referred to as the **kubelets component config**, which normally provides space for flags used in the cluster DNS IP addresses.

The DNS resolution system may differ in Kubernetes configuration flags when the paths of use are different from the intended. In this case, the kubelets are prone to fail when the nodes are configured incorrectly in the system. Users may intend to set up a metadata name as the default hostname using a personalized computer, but not a cloud provider. The **Hostname** overrides the default behavior, and more specifications need to be set where the Node name is said to be the same as the username. More importantly, kubelets are set to detect cRI runtime, and most developers used cgroup drivers to be secure and healthy when running kubelets. Users also need to specify different flags, depending on the CRI runtime. For instance, network plugin is used in Docker flags when one is used in the external runtime. In this case, users need to specify the direction of instructions such as: `-container-runtime=remote` directed towards the Endpoint: `runtime-endpoint=<path>`.

Kubernetes Proxy Service

The proxy services are strategically used to make each node available to the outside host. These kinds of services are made available by communicating with the etcd store, where the details and right values command are received and retaliated correctly to meet the component Master demand. In this case, the kubelets' processes are maintained within a specific state, and it works best under the S server node. Here, we are responsible for port forwarding and network roles maintenance. The network environment is always predictable, though they are isolated for accessibility, and proxy service is used to manage the pods on node, secrets, volumes, and health check-up of the system.

Basically, Kubernetes employ a combination of virtual network devices it normally allows, the pod running, and the communication sender and receiver of the network IP address. It includes exciting procedures that enable you to create a sustainable and durable system, due to its ephemeral nature. You can use an IP address at the Endpoint, though there are expected changes that may occur at the end when you want to access it. In this case, there are no guarantees that there will be no changes.

Many people will recognize this kind of problem as the old nature of Kubernetes, but it can be corrected through a reverse proxy or load balancer. People are known to log into the proxy and expect it to maintain the healthy servers as requested. The implications that normally arise are common in any system, though they need few corrections as per the needs of the technology. Developers tend to create a durable and resistant-to-failure proxy, and they do so by creating a list of healthy servers that are able to respond to any request immediately. Therefore, the designers can solve the problems by building the server with the basic platform requirements.

There are hypothetical clusters used to show the server pods how they can be communicated to various nodes. The developers provide clients with the platform to operate independently during the deployment; however, the too simple HTTP server created by the deployment platform normally responds to the 8080 port of the hostnames. These are run after creating the deployment by sending queries to various pod network addresses. Due to the presence of the client pods and the cluster that exists between the pods, one can send and receive a response within the network with much ease.

Components of Kubernetes Architecture

You will acquire a cluster if you apply Kubernetes techniques in any system application you plan to use. These clusters comprise of machines known as **nodes** that enhance the management of containerized applications run by Kubernetes. Most of the time, people tend to involve at least one master node in the application design; however, pods that are the components of the application are normally administered into the system by the worker nodes to create a conducive platform for system integration. The management of worker nodes created within the application and pods in a cluster are also used to provide master nodes with the greatest interface. At the same time, the multi-master nodes are made responsible for the provision of the high availability of system failover. Moreover, there is a list of components that you deserve to have for the working cluster of Kubernetes for the application components to be considered necessary and essential for use.

Critically, Kubernetes has a variety of master components that act as a control plane of the cluster to operate efficiently. The master components can be controlled on any machine, provided it be within the cluster that constitutes the whole system functionality. These components are as follows: Kube-scheduler, which is a master component that plays a major role in the administration of newly created pods that aren't assigned any node and identifies a node for them to run on; individual and combined resource requirements, which include basic equipment such as hardware, software, policy constraints affinity, and anti-affinity specifications; inter-workload interference; deadlines; and data locality.

The etcd is a highly available and consistent key factor used as Kubernetes' backing store for all cluster data. You need to have a backup plan for your data if your Kubernetes cluster applies etcd and its backing store. Official documentation can be used to derive in-depth information about etcd. With Kube-controller, the manager runs controllers where each controller consists of a separate process. All these controllers are compiled into a single binary to minimize complexity, and are categorized as follows: the node controller is responsible for sensing and responding when the nodes go down; maintenance and correction of pods are ensured by the replication controller; service account and token controllers produce accounts that are the default; and new namespaces are provided by API access tokens.

The key components of the Kubernetes cluster are made up of global decisions about the events that comprise of new pods used for deployments when there are unsatisfied replicas. In this case, the master components of the clusters are set in how we provide simplicity about the script, and the user container within the machines provides the master components required for building a high-availability cluster. On the other hand, the use of Kube-scheduler has a newly created pod in the system, whereby the ports are selected and run during the application development. Moreover, various factors are considered when deciding on the scheduling for a collective resource requirement, policy constraints affinity, and anti-affinity of the software specification on different directives of the system, without interfering with the deadlines.

Typically, the Kobe-controller manager, which constitutes of different processes, compiles with the binary of reduced complexity. This factor is composed of a node controller as the fundamental function for responding to other components when the nodes go down. On the other hand, the replica controller, that which is responsible for maintaining several pods, are used to control the objects in the system, which are done by the support of Endpoint control. The Endpoint control joins the services and pods together to create the service account for default API access.

Additionally, the cloud control managers usually interact with the underlying cloud provider and read a binary of Alpha features for the cloud controller manager. Here, there are specific controller loops configured in the system that are specific for starting the application. The external devices are flagged by the cloud provider to make it more controllable and accessible by outsiders. It also allows the cloud vendors and Kubernetes codes to evolve without any interference by any other vendor, which may trade in the market. In most cases, the core Kubernetes code is prone to derive the functionality from the cloud providers, and it is predicted that the cloud vendors will tend to maintain a specific function code to be used uniformly by all the components' functions. When that happens, the cloud control manager will be able to perform all the requirements of the Kubernetes.

On the other hand, the Kubernetes objects are used for obstructions in any state of the cluster. These are the changes made by the system to direct all instructions toward meeting the desired state of the objects. In this case, all the objects are maintained in the system, as per the specifications. If you want to create an object, there are specific requirements you have to meet, which are the **specs** and **status**. For the status, we need to manage all the updates following the desired state, whereas specs are provided by the Kubernetes to describe some of the component desires. For instance, if you want to run an image in many containers, you must modify the specs field. In this case, every object has a specific spec field where it is run to perform the desired task it was modified for in the beginning. Some of the specifications provided include the YAML file, used as the Kube-EPiServer to transform JSON, as per the API requests.

Pods are the basic components of the Kubernetes and are run logically in the computer. The center of attention is created by the pods' containers, which are orchestrated through various means in the inter-process communication platform. There is a local host system created by the containers to provide **pod love bubbles**, which are essential for Kubernetes. These components are used to create a namespace network it the same IP address run within a single container per pod. In most cases, the application may require a helper inform of proxy or pusher on different scenarios, especially when the first communication is needed through the primary application. A container as the array of several subfields where the pods are run is more essential for images spinning and argumentative commands than the entry point. Usually, all the objects are run through the container fields.

Cloud Controller Manager Manages Control

The cloud controller manager manages controllers that associate the cloud vendor's code and Kubernetes code to evolve separately from each other. Kubernetes depended on the cloud provider-specific code for functionality before its release of the system to the users. If it is to be provided in the future, the cloud vendors' specific code needs to be maintained by the cloud vendors themselves with coordinated support from the cloud controller manager, at the same time managing Kubernetes creates a platform for the user.

The Node Components

The following controllers have cloud dependency providers of the application and the user. The **node controller** is accountable for confirming the determination of the cloud provider in the cloud after it halts its response. The **route controller** is responsible for the construction of the routes in the underlying infrastructure of the cloud. Creating, updating, and deleting the provider of the cloud loan balances are the roles played by the **service controller**, whereas the attachment and mounting of volumes are conducted by the **volume controller** in such a way that the entire interactive platform is enhanced. Interaction with the cloud provider to orchestrate volume is also another role played by the volume controller.

The following are the **node components**, which manages running pods, running all code, and providing the Kubernetes' runtime environment. Running on each node in the cluster is an agent known as a **kubelet**, which ensures that all containers are running in a pod. It contains a set of **pod specs**, provided through various mechanisms and are liable in ensuring that those pod specs are healthy and running.

Implementation of cluster features is ensured by **add-ons** with the help of Kubernetes resources (deployment, daemon) and many others. The following are some of the selected add-ons. **DNS** is the containers founded by Kubernetes automatically consist of the Domain Name System (DNS) as a server within the Kubernetes on the computer. For that reason, **cluster DNS** is strictly required in all Kubernetes clusters, as many examples rely on them. Moreover, the cluster DNS is a DNS server responsible for serving DNS records for Kubernetes services. It is included with other DNS servers in the environment and other components within the system for clarity and flawless performance of the component.

The most significant objects in Kubernetes are the **pods**, and revolving around them are numerous objects called **basic servers**. Pods are for Kubernetes, whereas the rest of the objects are responsible for making the pods achieve their desired condition. Pods are a logical object responsible for running the Kubernetes containers, making them the center of attention. It is a logical object that manages one or more containers together on a similar network namespace: **inter process communication** (IPC). **Process ID** (PID) namespace also depends on the version of Kubernetes. The main objective of Kubernetes is to be a container orchestrator, so, with the support of these pods, orchestration is made possible.

Container runtime is the base engine that enhances the creation of containers in the node's kernel for our pods to run. The kubelet will be communicating with the runtime and will stop or spin up the containers on demand. Therefore, container runtime is required to enhance the spinning up of containers. Kubernetes' **deployments** are responsible for the definition of the scale that your application needs to run on by allowing you to set details for how you would prefer pods to be replicated on your Kubernetes nodes. They are also involved in the description of the number of preferred, identical pod replicas that will manage the desired update strategy used during updating the deployment.

Administrators and users of Kubernetes use the **Master server** as the main entry point, which will allow them to manage various nodes. It receives operations via HTTP calls and running command-line scripts, or through connection to the machine. In this case, Docker is the first requirement that assists in the management of the encapsulated application containers in a relatively isolated, yet lightweight, operating environment. Such an environment creates a platform through which all the essential communications are transmitted between the sender and the receiver.

Responsible for coordination of information to and from the control panel service is the **kubelet service**. To receive command and work, it has to engage in effective communication with the master component. Maintenance of the state of work and the node server is role played by the kubelet process in the whole process, and running on each code to make services accessible to the external host is the **Kubernetes Proxy service**. It is also responsible for forwarding the request to rectify containers and can perform primitive load balancing. It ensures that all the environments for networking can be easily speculated, readily available, and isolated at the same time, as well. On the other hand, restart policy creates a platform in which the Kubernetes creates a **zero exit code**, whereby either option is chosen within the on failure. When this incident happens, the containers are restarted to their default settings, the basic specs are declared within the container, and interaction with other objects is created within the Kubernetes components.

Chapter Three:
Kubernetes API Server

Characteristics of the API server

As depicted in the overview of Kubernetes, the API server is the gateway to cluster accessed by all users. The **API server** is used for automation, and it forms the largest part of the Kubernetes cluster. Normally, it is implemented on a restful API over HTTP and, by doing so, it is obligated to perform all the API operations backend it stores.

Kubernetes server is normally complex, but it is made easier by its use and management through various characteristics. Due to its persistent state, the API server is stored in the database located externally; it is stateless and can be replicated to handle diverse requests, thus enabling it to tolerate faults in the system. For this reason, they are highly available clusters in the API servers, which are replicated three times on every entry. One can perceive the API server to be chattier considering the number of logs as per the output. Usually, it draws a single line for a request received we try to insinuate that critical log rolling is added to the API server, so it doesn't consume a lot of the limited space in hard drive. However, the API server logs prove to be more essential when one wants to understand the operating system of Kubernetes. For that reason, many people prefer that logs be transferred from the API server and aggregated to subsequent introspection mining the debug user, which is also referred to as **the component request to API server**.

There are various characteristics of an API server that need to be looked into by the user and the developers of the application to make it more stable and adaptable. Therefore, organizations usually accelerate the adoption of containers orchestrated to take the necessary steps in protecting the property of the computer infrastructure. To ensure that all these things are done correctly, some characteristics ensure that Google Kubernetes is secure.

Foremost, the capability to be upgraded to the latest version makes the API server more flexible and stable. The new security features do not only fix the bugs in the system, but it also makes a quarterly update that takes advantage of the upgrade, thus enabling users to run the latest and most stable version. Their system also allows the users to receive the latest release in the market to create the most recent patches—there was the discovery of **CVE-2018-1002105**, which was more flexible and stable. Though there is difficulty in upgrading the system annually, one should upgrade Kubernetes with the latest version every quarter, so they can make it much easier and more flexible at all times.

The API server is characterized by **role-based access control** (RBAC), which provides access to the Kubernetes API server. It is enabled by the default settings of Kubernetes 1.6, which are usually managed by the provider or the developer of the system. One can only upgrade the server once they have purchased it without changing the configuration. In some instances, the user will tend to double-check the system setting to change the configuration to its desirable state. Since the Kubernetes authorizations controller is normally in a combined state, both parties are ordained to disable the Legacy attributed based access control and enable the RBAC for it to work well. For that reason, one needs to enforce an RBAC once it is effective and ready to use. They need to avoid the use of cluster-wide Permission in favor of namespace-specific permission, which is where they should not give anyone a cluster-admin privilege, giving rise to the debugging. One only needs access to a case-by-case basis for security purposes. They can also explore cluster roles by the use of **kubecti get cluster role binding**, which is all in the form of the namespace used to check the special cluster-admin who has been granted access to the master group. In most cases, the users prefer to create a Kubernetes API server for individual access and grant permission for its site without much difficulty. For this reason, there is an over granting default account permission for the namespace. API server normally has an Auto mount service account token for easy access.

There is a use of a namespace in establishing security boundaries, which is an important component for isolating objects. The component provides a security measure that is essential for controlling and monitoring the network. In this case, the network policies are differentiated to different workloads, which are further separated into the different namespace. When a namespace is used effectively, one can easily check any non-default object in the system.

The API server is critically integrated into the separate sensitive workloads, which normally limit the potential impact on the compromises that may occur. The sensitive workloads are normally dedicated to a set of machines that reduce the risk of being accessed by outsiders. It, therefore, uses a less secure application that shares a container host. In most cases, the nodes' Kubelets credentials are normally compromised when they are mounted on the pods, thus leaking the secret.

There is more adversary to secrets schedule on many nodes, creating high chances of being stolen. Therefore, the API server uses more separate node pools to encounter further problems through the use of the cloud taints, namespace, or toleration.

On the other hand, there are define cluster network policies for how to enable users to control network access. There is a restriction on the containerized application, creating full control of the software, and the only thing needed by the user is the network that supports the resource. Most people prefer using the Google Kubernetes engine (GKE) for managing and opting for the network. In case you have an existing rolling cluster upgrade, one only needs GKE to restart the application to its default network policy for effective and efficient use. You would need to make a regular check on the cluster on which the network is running and redirect it to the Google container engine.

Additional API server runs on a cluster-wide pod security policy, which normally defaults where the workload is round on throughout the application. By considering the definition of the policy and enabling the security policy controller to run as per the cloud provider model, the application becomes secure. One may require all the deployments are a drop in the network's raw capabilities, ensuring that there is proofing of attack that may occur. In this case, the system is made secure and stable by all means. The provider and the user also have peace of mind on the performance of the Kubernetes, and there is a Harden node security, which ensures that the host is secure and configured correctly. It usually creates a benchmark of checking the configuration against the CIS, which is a better automatic checker. This normally keeps the standard with the performance required by the application to keep up with the market mechanism. To add, there are a network control access ports that block unnecessary access to the application server, including 10250 and 10255 ports which can create limited access to the Kubernetes API server at any given point. Most malicious users, like cryptocurrency miners, usually tend to corrupt the system through the use of different figuration when there are no proper authentication measures put in place. Also, there is minimal administrative access to most of the Kubernetes clusters nodes and no need for involving different uses in protecting the application.

The developers usually ensure that there is a turn on the audit logging used in monitoring the anomalous of the unrequired API calls. These are used when there is a failure in the authorization application software, whereby the entries of the status messages are denied. Moreover, there are high chances of creating reducing credential abuse, which makes the software insecure and unsuitable for users. The Kubernetes providers usually make sure there is a secure container for all ongoing communication in the API server through the use of GKE in securing the data. To secure all the data and necessary information required by the user, the provider normally creates a notification alert on any failure that may occur due to infringement of the application basics.

Pieces of the API server

The Kubernetes involve key functions that are integrated into different pieces of the API servers, such as API management, request processing, and internal control loops. In this case, we are going to look at each component and how each one affects the entire software.

API Management

Since the fundamental role of the API management is to service individual clients, the process is more tedious and it involves more processing for different requests. In this case, there is more to the API requests, whereby the client request must be met at all levels. One should always remember that the HTTP request is the same as the API server request made by the Kubernetes, and the difference in these components must be accessed through various sources for accurate information. In most cases, one can intend to employ a minikube tool to access the local Kubernetes cluster. Moreover, there is the `curl` tool in exploring the API server when running under different proxy mode for authentication. On the other hand, they can deny unauthorized accessibility through the use of **localhost: 8001** through various commands.

The API uses a support system, in which the connection is pulled into the data, which is the integral pattern of the product. In this case, customers are not allowed to access a particular piece of data by giving the recommended answer to access the API server. One should always remember that API is like USB ports; the information can be accessed from the given point. Although it is a bit different, this API service is the help desk customer care in a foreign country, where they would provide all the program information needed by the foreigner in the form of codes. By doing so, chances of replicating the program are entirely limited, and the codebase is not replicated. In such cases, the data for programs are available outside the server. The most interesting part of API server is the coding language used to communicate the program to the users. In this case, the programmer may decide to expose the data to the outsiders or hide the data from an external attack.

When a portion of the language code is exposed to outsiders, there is a great chance that the externalist can hinder the system functionality and another program can pull out data from the application URLs, all through the use of the client HTTP details. Special programs built on these URLs normally request data from the Endpoint turn and return the text to the computer's user. It also allows a user to request data from the provider for a given purpose. Usually, the computer tends to make things easier for the user in certain ways, such as invoice collection tasks from the customers. One can easily access the data in the company's invoice records, which is stored in the computer for further reference, and print them for audit purposes. These invoices are normally uploaded from the central database, and a developer can easily write a program that records the partner's name by using a simple program. The person who codes such programs normally takes less time to make things correct and accurate.

The person can hold data for a longer period before releasing it to their users, and once the server is running, it is later published for documentations through the endpoints of specific data. This documentation is used to tell the outside programmers about the internal structure of the data on the server.

The application programming interface has been in use for the last few centuries. Without protecting this kind of technology, the digital experience of the customers could not be the same as it is today, as it all depends on the information-rich marketing campaign. The continuous use of the mobile app for internal streaming operations has been enhanced lately through coding and other computing technology. Most businesses have invested in technology that embraces the API strategy through various platforms and, interestngly, the API system is a task that does more heavylifting on the web. All these are usually done by clicking on the computer to make an order for items, like pizza books, songs, and downloading software. A person may not notice the working of the API server because it works in the background of the interaction that we want on the interface. In the case of a user is searching for a book in a store or a hotel when traveling, the user is doing these via online sites. The engine makes work easier for everyone who intends to use it correctly without compromising the intended purpose. With the second example, the information is integrated from different hotels into one database system for an easier search, and the delivery is always met through different criteria set by the system. The API servers run like a messenger between database applications and devices to deliver the intended information. The price of API as acronym character is the application programming and interface.

The application typically accounts for a complete transaction between the system and the user. ATM, for instance, is an application whereby the account holder can access an amount in the account when they want to withdraw money, without going to the bank. The interface provided by the ATM communicates with the user in accessing the bank details, and the user doesn't need to go straight to the bank to access the money while using the ATM, reducing the waste of any time. The app input and output create end-to-end user accessibility to solve specific problems, and the server software serves as a funnel service database in which the interaction is made.

The other piece is the programming interface that communicates with the bank during the transaction. It serves as the programming engineering part of the software application, and it is normally recorded by the programmer to act as the intermediary between the provider and the user. In this case, it provides an intermediary between the bank and the bank holder, whereby they can interact freely without meeting at a certain point. The service interface translates input into output, in which the bank holder order requests to the provider, related to the ATM interface through cash to bank database. If you have enough money in the account to withdraw, the software responds as per the request and it grants permissions to the ATM to dispense the specific amount and update the balance appropriately. As we all know, the software only responds to the request made by the user, which is how the server works.

On the other hand, the **user interface** (UI) **crest platform**, in which one interacts with the application. To derive from the same example of the ATM, the user interface is the screen keypad and cash slots to which the user has a clear access, and they can create an input responded by the output that occurs when the money is delivered. The interface provides a platform in which the user can enter the PIN, then punch the amount they intend to withdraw, after which the cash is paid out by the system. It is through these interfaces where the user can communicate with the machine and receive an immediate response through the action done by the machine. Therefore, API server works the same way as the ATM, but only in how it uses a software interface. In other words, the API server can access all the current data of the software. In this case, the ATM is the end-user of the API, where customers can press a button to command a request more digitally.

The website uses a URL address on the web browser and pulls up the appropriate request. The API server normally begins the transaction request through a shared currency asset, as per the company's needs, and it can be integrated between individuals or teams to external developers where they buy pieces of code, data points, and software accessed. The company normally owns the rights to share the information, and the API acts as a gateway to the server, where it provides a point of entry for the audience. Developers use this software to build on the application, and the software critically filters all the asset objects needed to secure itself from outside intruders. The end-user rarely uses the API server for their purposes, since the application is normally accessed by the developers and the providers make it difficult for the end-user to access it at any point. However, when they do get access to it, they usually have incomplete information or data needed for access. In this case, the assets tend to take into account which commands are more creative for implementing data that was previously used in the business to gauge the owner's assets. For this reason, the developers tend to reuse previously used software components to create the codes for the software.

The **resultant data** is connected to the server application to provide a richer and more intelligent experience for the users. This is what makes the API occasions more compatible with different devices of the operating system, as it creates a seamless experience to the user. The beneficiaries of the apps' the end-user, who is more flexible to different applications, creates a social profile to interact with the third party. In a layman's language, the API acts as a doorway through which the user can get into specific information when accessing a given asset. It seamlessly creates a communication channel through which the flow of data is enhanced in the software application. The developers can create an application in a more diverse format such as wearable, mobile application, desktop websites, and among other options through which an interaction engagement is enhanced. The platform enables the developer to create a rich user experience application, and it also creates a platform, whereby the developer can create an application of another app for their entire business through web applications such as Zapier, Hootsuite, and IFTT. These were created to provide leverage to API when writing application code. Though other applications act as core functionality during development of all business-crucial apps, they are intentionally used for reusable purposes in the technology.

The API normally acts as a universal plug, which can be compared to two different key holders who speak the same language. It does not matter for many people, as long as they get access to what they want in the application. For instance, many people look to gain access through various country code sockets. The standardized access creates a lot of flexibility in the system, and anyone can access it without any regulations.

API Management

The typical function of API is to respond to the client request by processing all the inquiries in the system through an integrated interface. The request is made by the HTTP server respondent to the API interface through a good description by the client in the communication channel, provided by the application. In this case, the request must be articulated well, so the client-server responds appropriately. One can decide to use the existing Kubernetes cluster to access all the tools of the application by using various system commands to convey the message data.

API Paths Used by the Application

For every request made by the API server, there is always an existing restful pattern that follows to define the HTTP pattern of the request. Therefore, the Kubernetes request follow-up defines that path in the form of the prefix: `/api/` (usually integrated into the API groups). However, the application has two different paths through which the Kubernetes did not originally exist, so the original call objects are like pods and the service is maintained under `/api/`, in absence of the API groups. In this case, they follow the prefix of: `/apis/<api-group>/` path. Here, the job would be part of the batch under the `/apis/batch/v1/`.

Request Management

Since the main purpose of the API tool is to receive and process requests made by the users, the Kubernetes tends to process all the calls in the form of the HTTP requests and communicate directly to the user. The requests can be received from various components of the application or directly from the end-users of the Kubernetes server differently. For this reason, there are different types of requests that are integrated into the data application. These broad categories comprise of the **GET**, **LIST**, **POST**, and **DELETE** component requests.

GET requests specific resources that delegate the information, as per the request relied on the path followed. For instance, the HTTP can get the request to follow a specific path like `/api/v/`, followed by `namespace/default/pods` and the data later retrieved in the pod name *foo*. Such channels are crucial for the system's functionality and stability, for the users and the providers.

LIST takes a more complicated route, though it as straightforward as far as the requests are concerned. It comprises a collection of GETS, where LIST requires several diverse requests made in the application HTTP through a given path to complete the circuit. For instance, the request may follow the path of `/api/namespace/default/pods`, which are later retrieved in the namespace collection data. In other instances, the LIST may opt to specify the query label used during the request process. When such inquiries happen, the resources that are used in making the query are repeatedly returned.

When it comes to the POST request, the resources created in the application regenerate new posts paths used to respond to different inquiries of the users. The provider has a platform interface through which the path resource created is retrieved in `/api/v/namespace/default/pods`. In this case, the resources are used to update the specific resource path, which takes the direction of `/api/v/namespace/default/pods/foo`.

Another type is the DELETE resource, which takes time to delete the request made in the application. It normally takes the path of the requested resource, like: `/api/v/1/namespace/default/pods/foo`, as directed by the system interface. The changes made by such requests normally alter the interface of the system permanently. This means that the request is deleted for good and cannot be retrieved for future use when the developer requires it.

Therefore, it is worth noting that the content of the resource requests is the text-based JSON (`application/JSON`) through a recently released application of the Kubernetes to support the protocol buffers' binary system coding. In most cases, JSON is preferred by many people, based on how it is friendlier to the user and allows for enhanced user readability, thus allowing for the creation of debugging traffic on the internet. This traffic is suitable for linking the client-server and provider server for easy access and communication basis. For instance, `attach` and `exec` commands are used in the system to create such requests in different sections. Though they are normally expensive and difficult to analyze in the language of the application, some common tools are used to buffer the protocols of introspects like `curl`, which is likely to ensure the greater performance of the application. Additionally, some of the content requests are made by the websocket protocol for a streaming session of the system server. In this case, the protocol used is the `exec` command.

Life of Requests

The life of a request is determined by the API to sever the ability to deliver the client command and process different requests as required. The server takes the processing of the requests as the main functionality of the Kubernetes.

Foremost, we intend to stand with the authentication stage, where the requests are processed for authentication, and identify different resources associated with the data request. It also engages different modes of data establishing identity in the application, which normally comprise the bearer tokens, client certificate, and the HTTP basics during the authentication process. Generally, clients place their tokens and certificates for system authentication and, by doing so, some of the HTTP basics are discouraged. In other instances, the pluggable identity establisher is used for authentication, and these involve several plug-in implementations that normally identify the provider or user remotely. It may include the support for the OpenID connect through a certain protocol provided by the application's built-in codes. Also, they may include the Azure active directory identity plugin of the API server for verification of the compiled client details. It sorts all the clients according to the specifications and command-line tools with a rough version that supports the authentication protocol.

The API server usually supports the authentication configurations of the webbook-based authentication decisions, delegated to the outsider bearer. It normally validates the bearer token, which runs the authentication information from various servers. It is quite astonishing that the basic request management secures the server for efficient and effective usage.

After authentication, the data is moved to another compartment of the server for authorization of the identity entered in the application circuit. Every request follows the Kubernetes' traditional RBAC model, whereby the request is remitted for appropriate association and alignment with the response. The Kubernetes RBAC is rich in complicated requests, from diverse topics used to categorize every request, to a desirable compartment for adoption and realignment. The major role of the RBAC is to determine whether the request can meet different criteria for identification and conformity. In this case, the verb conformity is integrated and the identified role is processed by the HTTP 403, as it returns the response and creates a new avenue for the request created in the first place.

The next step is the admission control, which is entitled to the request authentication admission control role. It clarifies the viability of the request, recognizing whether it should be allowed to occur in the system. All the verification details are examined in the control admission compartment, and it is based on the HTTP properties' request. It follows the method, header, and path criteria to determine whether the request is well-formed in the control admission compartment of the application. It also applies a modification of the request processed, according to the requirement of the standards to evade the security attack. The pluggable interface defined in the system is integrated in such a way that all the requests' criteria are met with the defined specifications.

If the admission control encounters any error after the authentication, the request is automatically rejected and the provider has to reenter the correct authentication identity. However, when the request is accepted by the API server, it is inverted and used the way it would be without further correction. No alteration is allowed after it has been allowed in the system through the admission protocol created. The serial of the output is used to verify the previous details, which have been entered in the application server. Since the admission control has a pluggable mechanism, it supports a wide variety of functionality in the API server. Usually, it adds the default value to objects through a forced policy and a certain object label. In this case, the additional content is injected in every container of the pod for a service mesh and transparency. The generic property of the admission control requests is to be integrated correctly in the API server through the use of webhook-based admission control.

Ultimately, the request is subjected to the validation criteria compartment, which occurs after the admission control. The validation is made through the Webhook-based validation process, which has an additional object for request validation. One merely needs to acquire a wider knowledge of the cluster state through an implemented admission controller. Moreover, the crucial role of the validation request is to ensure that all the specific resources included in the admission control are valid and viable for further verification when the need arises for such action to be taken. For instance, it normally ensures that the name of the specific object of the company is the same with the provided details in the DNS server, where the name of the server is further submitted to the programmed Kubernetes server. Critically, the validation is used to conform to the defined resource implementation criteria of the DNS server.

Debugging API Server

Typically, understanding the API server implementation process is crucial, as it has a great impact on more than anything else in the Kubernetes management; although, one only needs to debug compatible objects that are in line with the API server, which is commonly achieved through audit logs written on the server. In most cases, there are two logs, normally used by the log stream to serve as the API server exports. They include the basic or the standard logs, which are targeted for what capture state requests are made on and how it tends to affect the whole system. The changed API server is alternated through logging, which is turned on specific problems that tend to affect the server at some point. These problems usually alter the efficiency and effectiveness of the whole system, eventually making them ineffective and invalid if not debugged in time.

By default, the request made in the API server is sent to the server logs for verification and validation before it is passed to the next level. These logs normally contain the client IP address, which is passed through a code of request to the server. In the case of any unexpected error, the server tends to panic and respond undesirably, indicating that there is a problem in the log given by the client. The panic tends to return various and many errors, up to 500 log errors. For instance, `[6803 19:59:19 929302 1 trace.go:76]` is traced to the other code, which is then verified for errors that may exist in the system. In this case, the log starts with the timestamp when the logline is omitted, which is later followed by the numbers that were initially omitted in the application system.

Audit Logs

The **audit log** is used for administration recovery of the omitted data, which was assumed when making the request. It may arise from the client's interaction, which is prone to derive the current state of the server. When the Kubernetes server is corrupted, it creates a complete error, which may prove difficult to recover from if not monitored carefully. The audit logs tend to pose questions to the client or the user to verify and validate the data correctly. For instance, a question seeking an answer to the current replica set to the scale to 100 is created for verification. The system may also pose a question, such as who deleted the pod. Compared with other replicated questions to validate the application viability and validity, the audit logs contrarily possess a pluggable backend, on which

71

the supposed logs are written for further verification and clarification of the logs entered.

Generally, the Kubernetes logs are written to files, thus differentiating them from other application audit logs that may not be written in file format. In most cases, they are written in webhooks for easy accessibility and use, where they would not be interfered with by other system factors. In either case, the JSON objects are structured in the audit event to a k8.to API group. In such cases, the auditing itself is configured into a policy object in the API server group, which allows specified rules to be remitted for use in the audit log. To add, there is a room for activating additional logs in *github.com/golang/glo* leveled logging, which is a package for logging in the API server in form of ...v flag, extensively adjusted to logging verbosity. Generally, Kubernetes are modified for creating a set log verbosity when specific problems are analyzed. When that is done, one can easily raise the logging level to see possible spam messages.

Chapter Four:
Kubernetes Load Balancing, Networking and Ingress

Kubernetes Load Balancing

Load balancing is the effective network traffic distribution in backend services within the Kubernetes server, and it aims to maximize the system scalability. It forms a strategy in which there is a variety of load balancing in the external traffic pods, with each having different tradeoffs. Foremost, there is load balancing that uses kube-proxy, whereby the Kubernetes cluster is sent to the component services. The **kube-proxy** is a somewhat confusing concept, but it should not be contradicted with the IP for service via iptables rules. The architecture of the Kubernetes normally adds complexity to routing in the way we go about it, which creates a latency for each request during the validation of the code requests of the client. The latency of the system normally grows with the number of service requests made by the client or the provider. The kube-proxy routes comprise of **L4 (TCP)**, which does not necessarily fit with today's application-centric protocols. For instance, most clients are prone to connect to the backend, in which the request is made per minute by sending the other 100 requests per second.

Therefore, the use of the kube-proxy simplifies the entire process and makes the load balancing easier and more efficient. The default strategy of delegating the Kubernetes makes the automatic load balancing of the Kubernetes via another service or through various ambassadors through a balancing mechanism.

On the other hand, there is also **L7 round robin load balancing**, which uses a **multiplexed keep alive protocol** of the Kubernetes servers in the form of gRPC or HTTP through a round robin algorithm. One can also use the API gateway of the Kubernetes in form of the ambassadors through `bypass kube-proxy`. Here, the routing traffic of the Kubernetes is made to cooperate in more direct pods. For load-balancing purposes, the ambassadors are built on a more fundamental envoy proxy in the L7 proxy. In every gRPC, the available pods are balanced in how they do not cause any harm or danger to the system. Furthermore, the load balancer uses a unique approach of getting the Kubernetes Endpoints API, in that it tracks the pods available in the application. In case a request is made concerning particular Kubernetes services, the load balancer tries to use its round robin technique to engage the pod's requests for a given service.

The Kubernetes can still use the ring hash for load balancing purposes and create a strategy between different pods and a hashing algorithm. Most of the clients have to send requests to different pods and create a strategy for balancing the load in the application system; however, the ring has an approach that creates a tricky situation, in which all requests are handled in the same pod. It is always imperative that you create a session affinity to detect the client IP, which would ensure that there are many diverse criteria on balancing the intended requests from the clients and the providers.

The **ring hash approach** is normally used to maintain the client state in the form of shopping cart services. In this case, the provider or the developer would route the client to a given pod, so they do not need to be synchronized on a different system. The user needs to get the client data pod, as per the request, and increase the probability of cache hits that may happen in the application; however, it may be more challenging for a person to trade off with the right ring hash, which distributes the load between the backend servers, thus eliminating more loads and creating a clear measure that is equated to the right procedure. Additionally, the cost of computation is made by the hash requests toward achieving a particular scale.

On the other hand, the developers of the Kubernetes may employ a **maglev**, which would behave like the ring hash in balancing the load. The hashing usually has a consistent algorithm developed by Google, and they are faster compared to the ring hash algorithm. They minimize the memory footprint of the hash table lookups. In this case, the algorithm of maglev generates a large portion of the lookup tables in the CPU processor to clear the cache. However, the maglev usually has an expensive tradeoff for the microservice trade offs. In other words, generating the lookup table in the node may fail and when such happens, and the node may create an expensive notch that would become more complicated. As per the spherical nature of the Kubernetes pods, it may become more difficult for one to use the system or the application more realistically. For a different reason, one may create a consistent hashing pod used for balancing the application details, and the maglev is taken as a benchmark for load balancing the Kubernetes requests.

Load balancing is also created through "**learning more**," which is a networking implementation in Kubernetes. Most engineers are more limited by the load balancing approach of learning more. According to Matt Klein, the introduction of the load balancing and proxying make the allegations clear and creative for how the networking Kubernetes are balanced. Most organizations have taken into account the use of Layer 7 to load balance the ingress traffic in the application system; in this case, the use of Twilio, Geckoboard, and Bugsnag. Besides that, the

Kubernetes may intend to use the ambassador API gateways to build on the envoy proxy in an open-source to support all the load balancing methods in the Kubernetes system.

Kubernetes Networking

The application was built and run on a different platform distribution over a cluster of machines, and it's from this distribution that makes the networking nature of the Kubernetes central and the deployment of the application. For one to understand the networking nature of the Kubernetes, he or she needs to know some of the fundamental factors entailed in the Kubernetes' running. These will enable one to monitor and troubleshoot the software application correctly and ensure that the Kubernetes are running smoothly when installing in the system.

However, networking entails a lot of technological space, through which the advancement is made daily. For this reason, people need to become familiar with the landscape and have a conceived notion of the networking task of the application by developing new concepts of the technology. However, there are more old and new concepts incorporated in the system functionality, which one needs to understand and fit based on the needs of the technology, specifications, and computer needs. In this case, non-exhaustive concepts can be engaged in the concept to arrive at the desirable state of the Kubernetes' networking in every system, as required. These may include IP forwarding, a virtual interface, namespace, and network address translation. In this article concept, the intention is to demystify the Kubernetes' networking nature by discussing the dependable technology involved in the networking of the application.

The Kubernetes are opinionated to the pod's functionality to ensure that the networking system is enabled, and it comes with different requirements to make a lot of work when implemented. It is worth noting that the pods' communication is made without creating an additional network address translation with other pods in the system, in order to make it work as required. Also, nodes are designed in such a way that they can communicate to pods without involving the NAT. In that case, the developers insinuate that the IP with which the pods identify themselves are not always the same and, to some extent, they would differ from one pod to another. However, there are some constraints involved in the implementation of the networking model of Kubernetes, which must be observed in the system modification. There is **container-to-container networking**, which is involved in the system implementation, and **pod-to-pod networking**; involved at the same time, pod-to-pod networking created in service networking forms an internet-to-service networking connection in every sector of the Kubernetes concepts.

As we get into the container-to-container networking, there is the communication of virtual interaction, directly with the Ethernet device, to make the whole networking concept be the way it has to be at the end of the model implementation. As a matter of fact, the situation tends to be more subtle when incorporated into the system.

The Linux communication process network namespace provides its users with a more logical networking stack embedded in its routes, firewall rules, and other network devices that are created in the system. There is a provision for the namespace network stack, which provides a new networking strategy. On the other hand, the Linux users can be networked back to using a single IP command. There is also a networking strategy for how the Kubernetes are run and how they incorporate all the created request handling concepts in the application network. There are other forms of the namespace in the route created by the networking process form `ns1` which is extended to $ `IP netns add ns1`. Additionally, the namespace created in the application has been established from `/var/run/netns`, which persists on the namespace process.

There is a list of namespaces available for the network listing, under which all the commands are based to ensure that the process is smooth and as per the agreed conditions established by the providers and the developers of the software. For instance, the provider may intend to use IP command to create a suitable network for the users: `&` is `/var/run/netns, ns1, & IP netns ns1`. These are created to ensure that the networking process is established. There are defaults, and Linux assigns the root network namespace where there is access to the external world.

When rooting the network namespace in terms of Dockers, there is a way that the modeled group containers shares the network namespace as it is created. In this case, there is the same IP address on the space assigned in the network namespace to the pod, within the pod. There is a way the pod is levied via the localhost, which resides within the namespace network of the application. The pods and the virtual machine are incorporated in the network, in which the system is routed and how it is run to ensure that all the processes are created in the implementation using the Docker in the pod container. In this case, the network namespace is focused on the app container, where things are user-specified and the namespace, Dockers, is created in such a way that it is routed to `Dockers-bet=container;` function. There is also a pod made up of various Docker containers, to an extent they share within the namespace. When networking in the application, the pod is accessed through a wide volume with defined pod parts, which is normally made available and created in each application filesystem, making it operate.

Pod-to-Pod Networking

The Kubernetes application creates a pod, in which the IP address communicates with other pods in the IP address, where there is a great use of the networking concepts to make either the impact or difference in the usability of the Kubernetes. In this case, the main concern is to understand the way pod-to-pod communication is being done and how they are achieved in the end. The communication is normally done through a real IP address, which is deployed on the physical node implication and cluster surrounding the entire event implementation. The node cluster creates or revolves around the network of the Kubernetes cluster in a way that makes the communication created and implemented at different levels. To understand the concept, one needs to have a coherent working experience with the same machine to avoid any scenarios that may give rise to internal concern complications or externalizing the node communication.

Basing on the pod's perspective, there is always an Ethernet namespace that ensures there is a communication network namespace within the node network created in the system. These pods normally exist within the Ethernet namespace, whereby the communication is enhanced through various network nodes within the application.

If there's a need to connect in the namespace network, there is an assigned side of route network analysis, which ensures that all other pods are networked within the application. In this case, each **virtual Ethernet pair** (or **veth pair**) part works like connecting a patch cable, which allows traffic to flow within the node cables. In most setups put in place by the providers or developers of the system, there is a veth pair created in connecting with VM routing namespace. When pods are set up in the network namespace, it is believed that they have their own internet devices to connect them to various IP addresses. For that reason, the roots can communicate with each other within the system and ensure that all the communication networks are bridged. Here, the pod communicates to each other pod through the namespace created in the application network. In other words, the **Linux Ethernet bridge** is a virtual and more complicated two-layer networking device incorporated in more network segments. It normally works transparently to connect different networks under one application umbrella. For one to maintain the bridge created in the application system, there is a need to conduct a forwarding table between the sources' aid in reaching the destination of examining the data packets. There's also a need to decide whether to travel or pass the packet in the network segment, whereby it would be used to connect the bridges between the two destinations. Developers use the betting code inform of data to create a drop on the MAC-address to describe the unique Ethernet devices in the network. The code created is unique, so it cannot be attacked by outside hackers. However, the bridges created are implemented through ARP protocols, which link-layer MAC addresses with other associated IP addresses within the system application. In case the dataframe is received by the provider or developer, the temperature broadcasted is connected to other devices in the system except that of the original sender, who only responds to the lookup table located within the frame store. It is worth noting that the IP address uses the lookup for traffic to be maintained within the packets.

On the other hand, there is a pod-to-pod in the same packet. In this case, the network namespace isolates all other pods within the networking stack. For this reason, there are virtual internet devices that connect the namespace to root the namespace bridge traffic between the pods on the same node. If illustrated well, the pods would create one of the internet devices, which is available by default to the other pods' Ethernet namespace. For pod 1, eth0 connects to the virtual internet that creates route namespace, which bridges and configures network segments. In case the pocket network reaches, the bridge makes it to one segment back to the packets. The traffic flow of the network default behavior is developed, as expected by the developers, and the networking in these pods is influenced by other factors within the system, like the respondents of the request made by the clients.

Kubernetes networking model is pivoted on how ports are made available or reachable by the IP address across the nodes. In other words, all IP addresses must be visible to other ports in the network to ensure that networking processes are per the designed model depicted by the developer in the initial stages of the development. For this reason, the IP address is made available and visible to other pods within the network, thus ensuring the communication network is effective and efficient. Though other problems may occur within the pod network on the route and in traffic between the nodes, there are big chances of eliminating possibilities by creating an effective traffic flow within the application.

We can now shift our Focus to the pod-to-pod lifespan of a pocket and how it affects the networking within the nodes in the application. Here, the main focus is on how routine traffic is made between the pods and different nodes. One should always focus on how networking in the Kubernetes model always requires structure within the IP pods, which should be reachable and accessible across the network. However, in most cases, there is not always specification for how they are being done, so the developers have come up with a way to make it work. In this case, important patterns have been established within the network. The nodes are typically designed in a cluster, in which CIDR does not specify the IP addresses within the pods and how they are being run on the node. This is all once the traffic has been established by the CDIR blocks, which are always the nodes responsible for the correct traffic pod flow.

It is very convenient to consider how the network is side-stepped and configured within the route traffic for the pod IPs. What is likely to publish the IP, which is responsible for the pod information directions in the network? Some of the issues involved in the network are considered when establishing the network; for instance, Amazon usually maintains container networking plugins that are connected with Kubernetes nodes and operate within the PVC of the Amazon environment using the container network interface of the company.

The container networking interface usually provides common API servers used in connecting containers to the outside network. As defined by the developers of the Kubernetes, pods are designed in a way that it can communicate with the network IP addresses and, for that to happen, the mechanism of actions is made transparent on each end. On the other hand, the CNI plugins, which are developed by the AWS, always try to meet the gap created in the application during the environment in which the networking is done through an existing IAM, VPC, and other security groups' functionalities, which are always rendered by the EWS. For a company to achieve all these, there is a need to establish networking interfaces scattered within the system's organization.

Kubernetes Advanced Services

The Kubernetes application is supported by important elements that make it suitable for scalable services to the users and the providers. The environment to which the application is mounted for microservices matters a lot, and it exists with specific tool features for effective use. Moreover, each part of the application is normally placed in a container, whereby the whole part is used for the Kubernetes purpose.

Every part of the application has ordained a place in the container, through which the Kubernetes application becomes scalable. It is clear that the use of the microservices and containers tends to facilitate the efficient flow of work, and the application itself becomes a CD/CI workflow engagement object. Each microservice container has its properties, which do not necessarily require the provider to update the entire system; it is usually updated separately. For this reason, the life cycle of the containers is short, especially compared to other applications that may use the same coding properties. This makes them more usable within the short limit and creates a market for future needs. The limitation created is not always desirable, however, as it depreciates the value of the applications supported in the technology advancement gap created when it does not last to meet the user's expectations. It is the durability of the application that makes it desired and wanted by many people and, when it is not durable, it becomes incompetent, in the part due to the developers and the service providers.

During the life cycle of the Kubernetes containers, the microservice property produces unexpected issues during the updates, and such issues can be avoided by taking measures on the rerouting and security of the application; although, some of these issues prove to cause many difficulties, in the part of user management. The users may end up corrupting the application when trying to correct errors that might emerge when performing a task.

In every application, there is a need to understand the dynamic IP allocation and how they are being managed in the application. Moreover, one needs to discover various primary challenges in service discovery, and how the services are being managed efficiently and effectively without encountering problems. These problem-solving techniques are useful to any developer who intends to secure the application software they have created and, by doing so, they are also able to provide the user with a more friendly application that cannot be infringed by the hawkers.

More importantly, one needs to understand the IP allocation, specifically with how Kubernetes addresses the pods and services to carry out its work. Though it is possible to define IP addresses, given that the services and pods have limits of their scalability on the Kubernetes environment, it is through these environments that defaults usually arise when there are new IP addresses allocated to the pods and services when restarted, and the system is unable to boot as required. For every cluster restart, there are new service possibilities created in the system, and for one to overcome the challenges, there are some methods that can be used. First, one can redefine the environment variables and services that tend to hinder application functionality. Similarly, one can look at the Dockers, which allow communication between the pods and to each other. It is through the Kubernetes where one can scan the environment variables and decide on which container to inject in the application.

In case you want services to run on different ports, you only need to run the `kubectl exec Memcached-rm58 env` command, which ensures there is access to **quick grep**. This service factor is used in revealing the service name and IP address of the user, and it also reveals the ports to which the service is assigned in the application. Therefore, it is the best way of managing the service discovery of the Kubernetes application.

On the other hand, one can consider the Kube-DNS to the rescue, which is normally considered to be a more efficient and effective method of the Kubernetes services for a long-run approach. The **Kube-DNS** is an add-on to the internal DNS resolver, and it acts on it appropriately. The Kube-DNS relies critically on the namespaces, whereby it eliminates the use of pods and other services within the application for it to function properly and based on the developer's description requirements. In this case, there is no configuration modification in the system, and the file clusters are taken into consideration and incorporated to allow the pods and the DNS-based services to be discovered.

89

Moreover, one needs to understand that the Kube-DNS is also inclined to support the DNS policies and DNS queries. For this reason, one can configure each pod in the application to follow different DNS properties, thus making the nodes run well. In this case, one can use private DNS zones to customize the flow of communication in the pods and how they relate to one another. Also, one can still take a further step in configuring the properties of different DNS and how they run in the nodes assigned to them in the application. It shows that there is a possibility of using the private DNS zones for customization and communication in the system. Typically, one can still use the DNS policies in a different step-by-step by following the pod-per-pod basis to suit the specific needs in the configuration system.

Furthermore, one can incorporate label and selector parameters to influence the pods, service performance, and communication networks created between each one to support the system capability. It is worth noting that the Kubernetes services normally support the discovery support, enhancing the control between the selectors and the labels in the pods. For instance, labels use the complex cluster management in the assigned components of the pods to create easy identification, and the parameters and the selectors are treated for ease in the working process of the Kubernetes. Various simple keys are always used by the parameters to create added metadata in the system, and these parameters do not actually affect the rest of the system environment; they normally create free labels and selector use across services and pods in the application. They even function well in the corrupt environment in which they may be subjected to work.

The next level can be a replication of the controllers used in the Kubernetes servicing system. The Kubernetes tools are available for the scalability of the system and can be easily replicated to maintain the availability and scalability of the system. In most cases, the developers tend to remove the pods and replicas in the system using one sweep as the action plan for improving its functions and abilities. Moreover, the use of the highly scalable service mesh makes the Kubernetes complete, and allows it to advance in the service discovery approach created in them. For instance, the AWS cloud map is normally integrated into the application resource to create a unique environment name. These environment names are automatically mapped in the system for scalability and request-response needed by the clients. The services are made to be discoverable in the system immediately once they are registered, and the process tends to happen as soon as the pods are launched in the application; once completed, it becomes available for scalability. The use of AWS makes the work easier and more discoverable by other service providers that use the same properties as that of the Kubernetes. The tool is part of the Amazon ecosystem, and it is used in traffic routes, calls, traffic balancing, and circuit breaking of the API system calls, which may be embedded into it by the providers. Microservices can also be used in the form of the app mesh for easy management and incorporation in the system, as it works well with other tools like the Amazon EKS, VPC, and IAM. These tools are important for application performance and security, which may be ignored by other users who do not know or understand their importance.

One should not forget that the Kubernetes service discovery is just one component that makes the containers more flexible and capable of performing its intended duties properly. Various approaches are used in the Kubernetes system, which inclines them to be more flexible and accessible by other components in the entire container. Through the use of standardization and the discovery of the system, the users can access and obtain information easily by using the Kubernetes application, which is both affordable and durable. Moreover, other running services can still be used in the API calls and data feed systems to ensure that all the requirements are met within the stipulated period. Data is fed into each other within the application, without the potential discrimination and disruption that may arise. In other words, the caylent providers of the DevOps created the high growth of the company's development and incorporated the Kubernetes developers to innovate more system analysis for further research. The information obtained from other companys' expertise is vital in creating an informed decision in the Kubernetes development. Along those lines, the use of cloud security, CI/CD pipeline, and cloud infrastructure were also adopted by other companies like DevOps developers and operators innovation.

Creating managing and consulting service providers ensures that the cost of operation is reduced as much as possible, and the option of hiring in-house is encouraged for the advancement of the Kubernetes operating system installed in user or provider computers. By scaling the team's and the company's human resource management, the company is prone to grow much faster.

Chapter Five:
Scheduler

Scheduling Overview

The schedule is majorly focused on pods created in the application, which has no nodes attached to it at that moment. For every pod that is used in the discovery of the scheduling system, each is responsible for finding the best node on which the pod will run. For this reason, the scheduler reaches the placement decisions, where it will account for scheduling principles. In case you need to understand how the pods are placed onto a particular node, there is a need to create a planning implementation by the use of the **custom scheduler**, which would help you learn how the scheduling is done. Hence, **Kube-scheduler** is normally preferred as the default schedule for the Kubernetes. They normally run on a control plane, which is designed in such a way that it enables one to navigate around the system, and it sometimes doesn't need to write down the components of the pods, for it is automated in the system without complication. For every newly created pod and schedule code created, the Kube-scheduler optimizes the node on which the pod will run.

However, the container has different requirements, whereby there is adequate resource allocation. In this case, every node needs to be filtered

94

according to specific scheduling requirements. In a cluster, feasible pods can meet the scheduling requirements of other pods and, in case there is no suitability of the nodes used in the application, pods will always remain and be scheduled until the replacement isdone by the scheduler. There is a way for the pod to function on a possible node and pick the node with the highest feasibility to run within the application. After that is done, the schedule server will notify the API server on the possible decision, which is made by the binding processes of the scheduler. However, there are some factors that need to be accounted for when making scheduling decisions. With finding the feasible nodes for the scheduler, there is also the need to recognize how each pod is created and modified on the application.

Some functions of the Kube-scheduler include selecting nodes for each pod for each two-step preparation. The overview of the Kubernetes scheduling has a scheduling overview that maintains call objects and aid in the display system, which generates the maintenance plan. Normally, it deals with the troubleshooting and maintenance of various aspects, which usually involve debugging pods and containers. These then involve the testing services meant for connectivity and interpreting the resource statuses of the nodes in the Kubernetes services. In this overview, the concept concentrates majorly on the app and cluster levels' maintenance, along with having much to do with troubleshooting, debugging, container testing, the etcd, and the Kubernetes control plane storage.

Users will encounter some problems when typing full commands in Kubernetes, which include the **kubect1**, as incorporated in the application. The autocomplete of the functions of the commands are integrated into the code application—for one to solve some of the system issues in the application, it would be through auto-completion of the kubect1 through Linux and bash shell. Some commands are used in the source completion bash for the operating system, where there is a documentation of the kubectl cheat sheet.

There is a need for removing a pod from the service, which is necessary for creating a good overview of the Kubernetes application, and there are more advanced pods that are used to create some of the outfits suitable for the endpoints in Kubernetes. To overcome some of these problems, the developers tend to relabel the pods in an **overwrite option**. By doing so, they ensure that there is the value of the run label and the service selector, which are normally removed in the endpoint lists. In one way or the other, there is a replica set over the pods that disappeared in the new replica.

In some instances, one can list the pods that are normally labeled with a **key run**, which include four pods run in the value of **Nginx** (run=nginx) integrated automatically. The label is automatically generated through the `kubectl run` command, created during the development. The format includes status, restart age, run: `Nginx-d5dc44cf7-5g45r 1/1`, and the running is created in `Nginx-d5dc44cf7-1429b 1/1`. These can later be exposed through deployment services and endpoints created by the corresponding IP addresses of the pods. Moreover, the service of the first pod's service traffic and the relabeling of the command created by a single command make the entire system work desirably. For a perfect Kubernetes working system, one needs to create an IP address that can manifest in all the pods, in line with the JSON and JQuery run query of the application.

The user can easily detect the pod's appearance and how they tend to exist in long service endpoints when accessing the cluster IP address outside the cluster when there are other internal services that may lead to some problems. In such instances, the developer creates a local integration of services without exposing it outside if one assumes that the services are made through the use of the pod's services, whereby one can enter nginc service in application software. However, all these services are unreachable outside the Kubernetes cluster, though one can still run a proxy on a separate terminal through a container known as the **localhost**, and they can specify the port on which the proxy is run through the port option. The original terminal, in terms of curl, accesses the application exposed by services that one is creating. In this case, JSON objects are used to represent the services in the Kubernetes' application. The user can access the entire Kubernetes IPA through the localhost using `curl`. Sometimes, when the user reacts according to the status of the resources or wire pod script automated environment in the Kubernetes application, the pods are incorporated in the nods modified, as per the specification.

In a cluster, the scheduling requirements are feasible in the nodes, in case the nodes are feasible and within the reach of Kube-scheduler, which tend to run on two application steps. These are done through filtering and scoring. On the side of **filtering**, the nodes are made feasible to the pods, which are integrated into **PodFitsResources** filter checks, the latter of which indicates whether the candidate is enough for the resource allocation, as per the specific requests. After following all these requests, the node list has some of the suitable nodes specified for some of the tasks done by the application pods in making the requests responsive, in case the pods are not ranked according to the list, schedulable in the software.

For the **scoring** steps, the remaining scheduling nodes are ranked according to the suitable nodes for the placement. In this case, the scheduler tends to survive each filter based on the active scoring tools and rules placed by the provider.

Ultimately, the Kube-scheduler usually assigns pods to each of the nodes, with the highest-ranking schedule as proportionate to the application. In any case, there is more than one node allocated to an equal score, and there are random Kube-schedulers selected in the system. However, there are default scheduler policies in the application that make it possible for the scheduler to allocate the requests to each pod, according to the capacity they can handle. In this case, the **PodFitHostPorts** normally checks if there are any available node ports, in terms of the network protocol used in pod requesting. On the other hand, the **PodFitHost** is used to check a specific node by integrating the hostname, as per the node application. Also, the PodFitsResources created in the CPU and the Memory direct to meet the requirements of the pods. In most cases, the pod's node selectors are added in the cluster for scheduling purposes, whereby the node labels are modified and created within the system.

Additionally, **NoVolumeZoneConFlict** is critically scheduled to evaluate the volumes of the pod request within the nodes, restricting the storage of the failure zone of the Kubernetes. In some instances, the use of the `nodiskconflict` is typically created in the scheduler to evaluate the chance that the pods can fit the node specifications, as per the volumes requests accorded to the application it already mounted on it to run.

In the filtering process, the developers usually create a **maxCSIVolumecount**, which is used to decide on the CSI volumes. These volumes are attached to a configured limit in the system for a clear request-response, which is necessary for the application's functionality. However, in case the node memory is subjected to pressure, there is a critical use of the configured exceptions, whereby the schedule is not depicted in the system, as required by the **chenodePIDPressure**. In other words, the nodes' failures are reported by the use of `checknodediskpressure`, which represents the filesystem made to be full or nearly full, with no reporting exception of the pods scheduled.

The Scheduling Process

The big data workload is created by **MapReduce**, based on the Apache Hadoop algorithms relying on the scheduling processes. In most cases, the **Hadoop**

Distributed File System (HDFS) ensures that the Hadoop in the node cluster is accessed in the dataset, and the architecture of the application is squarely focused because of its availability and reliability of the resources. The cloud foundation creates the Platform as a Serfice (PaaS) implementation within the Heroku, which has a sophisticated placement logic for the service schedule within the environment. In this process, the services are packaged and deployed in a VM to execute the task within the environment, on which it is placed to run by the physical host.

On the other hand, the rise in containers can lead the industry to reinvestigate the scheduler resources in the application system, which are made viable by the developers. It is done through scalability and simplicity as the key considerations in creating new schedulers of the application.

The traditional application is used through a handful of worker nodes through the many ways of user container management that was invented by the developers. To add, there is also more use of the modern incarnation of resources of the Kubernetes and mesosphere schedulers; in this case, the abstract within the infrastructure is made in such a way that the task is transparent to the users and developers of the application software.

The process of Kubernetes scheduling has become the most critical component in the cluster platform. These components are run on the master nodes, which are closely associated with the API server controller. For this reason, the servers are made to be responsible for the matchmaking of the node with the pod with which it is associated, and how they work together. Therefore, it is worth reading the Kubernetes architecture incorporation with other functions that are created within the system.

Furthermore, the scheduler is used critically to determine the appropriate pods, based on different resource factors that it is associated with in the application system, though it is always easy to influence the scheduler's affinity through the nodes it requires to implicate specific characteristics in the application system. For instance, the stateful pod tends to run on a high I/O database, which requests the scheduler node in the SSD storage backend in the CPU of the computer. There is a specific way that which the pods are placed to support the nodes for avoiding latency in the application incorporated for its functionality. In short, it is referred to as the **pod affinity of the Kubernetes**. Normally, it supports the schedulers during the placement of logics, which are completely driven by the third party.

Most technology advancement today uses the Kubernetes control plane for scheduling and in other functions like job management, which is distributed highly within the environment. These jobs normally include the deployment of the VMs placed strategically on the physical host, extending the control system, and even placing the containers in edge devices, whereby the schedulers within the wireless environment are supported.

The users can be allowed to run the VMs correctly by using the **kubeVirt**, which is the virtual management machine of the add-on Kubernetes, alongside the containers in OpenShift clusters or their Kubernetes application system. These extend the application functionality by creating the resources in the form of VMs and set through **Kubernetes Custom Resource Definition** (CRD) of the API server. In most cases, the KubeVirts VMs are run through the regular Kubernetes pods, where it accesses the standard pod networking and storage. These are managed through the Kubernetes tools in the form of the Kubectl.

The scheduling process normally involves an activity process that handles the removal of the running process in the CPU through the selection of different scheduling strategies. In computer coding, scheduling processes are the methods used to specify a bit of how some of the resources are assigned to perform a given task, and the scheduling process has become fundamental to computer science gurus. A set

103

of resources has become the most essential context resource allocation of the OS where jobs are simplified. In this case, the CPU core creates the foundation for scheduling tasks in the application and how it forms the greater part of the system.

Similarly, the OS within where the associating lines are responsible for code integration is threaded and semaphore created to make the scheduling task easy.

The distributed computing is expanded according to how the schedule task is distributed within the cluster of the physical machine. Initially, the distributed platforms such as DCOM, CORBA, and J2EE incorporated to form the scheduling components that had a lot of challenges within the cluster of application servers. Currently, the I Was control planes, commonly used by the Azure Fabric, Amazon EC2, and OpenStack Nova, are the scheduling virtual machines that are dealt with by hypervisors run on the physical host. Each VM is placed in an appropriate host, and the requested resources are included in the system application.

Scheduling Control

Most of the workplace competition has been heightened in recent years in the market, creating more avenues for project managers to have to have a critical bottomline on how to control the process.

However, business managers have come up with different strategies for creating a competitive environment in which the practices within the project are managed and controlled within the Kubernetes of the system. By injecting the best practices in the enterprise, the business can realize the profit desired by the organization at any point, without much interference. These are enhanced through a good communication network and coordination across the organizations' systems, whereby the various request is coordinated within the pods and nodes, thus developing a thorough flow of information across the network, without interference or hindrance from outsiders.

Before the Kubernetes extender, there was a need for one to understand the basics of how these schedulers worked, how they were supposed to be coordinated across different Kubernetes systems, and the way they met the requirements of the application. One needed to create a default starter that was within the parameters of the given Kubernetes and the needs they had to satisfy in the market to make it viable. In other words, the developer needed to watch the episerver, which were intentionally put in place to control the pods within the spec in the form of the node name in the internal scheduling queues.

For the control to be successful, one needed the following:

- To create a pod scheduling queue that is normally standardized to work within the scheduling cycle.

- To place more concern on the hard requirements that involved memory requests, mode affinity, CPU usage, and node selector in the pods API specs. After this phase, the node was calculated to satisfy the requirements within the node candidates.

- To retrieve the soft requirement of the API specs from the pods, which was applied as the default implicatioons put in place to aid the process became mandatory. This was with aid to control the scheduling process; in this case, each candidate node was selected to be the ultimate winner or the highest scorer.

- When apiserver was included in the control through issuing a bind call, the set node name was indicated, and the pods were scheduled within the pod setups.

- Within the official docs, it is pointed out that the config within the entry is where they are supposed to be in the system, and one should always aim at specifying the parameter of the scheduler used in the form of API perspective in the file configuration. These contain kubeschedulerconfiguration objects. They are in form:

```
#content of the fine within the
object to "—config"

Kind: Kubernetes configurations
scheduler

App version: Kubescheduler
```

These algorithm sources in the form of parameters are put in place to create the policy where the local file or the config map is created within the scheduler deployed in a more simplified and local file. The extended policy of the files is in the form of `/roots/schedulers-extent policy/config.json` which naturally contains the subjects of the `Kubernetes/schedulers /api#` policy. JSON can simply join the `Kubernetes/pks/scheduler` policies of the API server, integrated into the application system. Moreover, the form of JSON format in such a way that creates a `k/k#75852`. It is worth noting that these policies are registered with the default scheduler in the predicate and the priority phase of the extender services. These normally adapt to the basic business needs when controlled well in the application, and the main aim of such objects is to create the difference within the system.

There is a way that the extender in terms of HTTP(s) services are created in Kubernetes, and the program is written in any other language the developers chose to use to make it understandable and workable when integrated with the Kubernetes application, without any complications. These can be in the form of a Golang snippet and creating references in the following format:

```
Func main () {

Router ; = httprouter.new()

Router. Post("/filter", filter)

Router. Get("/", index)

Router.post ("/prioritize", prioritize)
```

In the next level, the scheduler filters the functions to the exact input type, which fits the extenderArgs with a returning scheduler API within the function, which is then further filtered in terms of the incoming nodes. As for the functions, the business nodes are filtered with the logics that judge the condition in which the approved nodes are placed in the system. In this case, the lucky nodes are approved and highlighted within the system application. Here, the source code functions are very important for the extended behaviors of the application, as it tends to explore the full extended config spec, which is later implemented in the bind and preempt functions in the application Kubernetes. However, there are some considerations worth noting and taken into account to deter it from experiencing some of the problems that can be prevented in a case, taken care of by the responsible individuals. These are to avoid regular failure of the pods, and which tends to occur when improving the system or during slight shut. It may further be caused by inaccuracy and negligence of the staff. By creating random logic, the numbers can be created in a running state of the Kubernetes system.

Limitations of the Control System of the Kubernetes Scheduler

In most of the scenarios, the scheduler extender can be a great option to use in the application, though there are some limitations within. These may include:

- The cost of communication where the transfer of data in the form of HTTPS between the scheduler extender and the default scheduler are not as efficient as required, due to various factors involved. The cost of performing serialization and deserialization are made within the system application.

- There are limited extension points noticed within the extenders and different phases in the filter and prioritization phases. These tend to

109

be in the middle or at the end of the phase of the application.

- There are nodes over the additions, which may be compared over the default schedulers for different reasons and passed as the default scheduler or for a different reason known to different people. It may prove to be risky in some ways, and there is no guarantee of passing the nodes to other requirements that may prove to be risky and unattainable in the scheduling process. In most cases, "preferable" means through the subtraction, which involves further filtering and these leads to more addition of nodes.

- Cache sharing, in most cases, involves the developer needing to adjust the fake cache used to connect it to another developing scheduler extender within the nodes. In practice, the decision is made by the scheduler default to make the right choice on which status to use within the cluster. In this case, the default scheduler takes the initiative to involve different and systematic decisions on the correct cache to use, whereby some of the built-in application defaults are maintained.

- There are some principles considered when controlling the scheduling process, which is normally overlooked and should be accounted for at any level of the Kubernetes developments. These can be seen as the guiding principle of the application software development and control measures.

- The development of the scheduler control needs to be responded to; not only viewed on the side of development. In this case, one should not control proactively, but act quickly by considering the changes that may impact the complete schedule.

- The control schedule can deal with the stakeholders' approach, where the guidance of the work is greatly considered and the managers of the project are left with the priority to accomplish other work pending, following the durations the work is assigned.

The next step involves knowing the actual performance to be taken by the schedule, which is essential in the working performance. It normally permits the schedule manager to adopt a diverse project schedule, which usually has adjustments to be made, depending on the required modifications of the application system.

Moreover, there are techniques used by the project schedulers to control the scheduling process of the entire project. These processes may be more diverse and, in many ways, the project schedule creates an avenue in which every process is made suitable for the flow of events or the query responsiveness by the pods and nods.

In the initial stages, the earned value management is utilized by the schedule variance and performance, according to how the index in which it is employed in the schedule changes and the scope is created. On top of that, one can have an essential schedule control for the schedule variation that needs a corrective measure or action within the limit. There is a probability of interruption of the project that may create a negative impact, thus creating a floppy situation that needs immediate action. When such events occur, there is a need to take the proper measures to correct the situation before it goes out of hand.

Also, creating criteria in which the critical chain within the schedule can be allowed through a comparison of the defensive methods are enhanced. By doing so, the delivery process can be aided in how it helps the regulation of other factors that tend to affect the scheduling process are dealt with within the time speculated. It is worth noting the difference, which exists between the buffer remaining and that which is required by the application to take appropriate measures to correct the situation.

On the other hand, measurements of the schedule utilized during the performance and the amount of variation involved depending on the schedule baseline must be considered. In this case, the aggregate float in terms of variance is more vital in the module assessed than the project performance.

For one to accomplish all these, there is a need for performing agile project management methodologies that have been adopted by several organizations that need to access the system by combining different factors. These are done through engaging the traditional project management skills combined with modern skills integrated into the management of agile projects:

- The indicators provide different control schedulers, which are incorporated in the operation for an efficient flow of work.

- It involves improvisation of the corrective process required for organization demonstration.

- Restructuring the rest of the work design under the scheduling process.

- The project delivery rates are regulated by the projects through approval and acknowledgment as it is emphasized.

- The criteria requiring that changes are managed as they happen.

Ultimately, the schedule control denotes that the actual project execution involves the comparison of the schedule, with other projects rendered within the project integration. It normally checks whether the actual remedial are within the venture track and includes the few metrics involving the evaluation of the project performance. It also involves a change in the essential data and control in the application process.

Typically, the concept involves the utilization of the management value and how each idea is ascertained by evaluating every project's performance. In every case, the data of work, schedule predictions, and demand changes are made essential for the control process of the schedulers. The control schedule is incorporated in the project management by involving monitoring of the status and activities that normally relate to a particular project. Apart from monitoring the status, it also creates a platform through which a project processes the management schedule according to the plan of achieving the set of objectives for the organization. By comparing the project baseline and the progress of the project against the manager's determination to achieve a particular project activity with proper scheduling, the controllers or managers of the firm create a platform through which they ensure that everything is as per the schedule. By doing so, the project managers can plan on corrective and feasible measures, through which they take their actions in the best baseline schedule. This reduces the risk of delivering the products and services of lower quality or quantity.

The control schedules are always part of the monitoring process, through which the project managers change and adjust to the corrective control measures that would be appropriate for the company. It should be noted that changes are not created, but instead acted upon and controlled, as per the specifications on which it is run within the application.

Another aspect of the schedule process is management of the customers' or stakeholders' expectations, which are done through engaging the customers' expectations and activities to be taken into account. These strategies are developed until the project is completed; therefore, it is important to create a platform through which the schedules are performed and managed by the control team. The actual performance of the schedule is noted to ensure that the integrated change control process is intact, based on the specifications of the organization and the activities and goals they wish to complete and achieve. The performance dissidents are approved using the **performing integrated change control**

process, which determines the status of the project. It is normally done through prioritizing conducting reviews and determining the work plan remaining.

In most cases, one can opt to use the schedule baseline to align the stakeholder's interest with the project outcome. On the other hand, one can use what developer schedule to manage important project activities efficiently and let the stakeholders of the project take control and care of the old project.

Record and schedule the project tool used instead of the baseline schedule when managing the intended project. Additionally, the project schedule management is also incorporated in the scheduling process; a potent aspect of service within the timeline of the project.

Ultimately, the schedule is used to see the project outcome, which is dependent on the management skills offered by the managers.

There are various ways that the catcher, caches, and callbacks are arranged to perform, depending on the functionality and scalability of the Kubernetes. In some cases, CoreOS is used for improving the schedule performance and reducing the controlling nature of the Kubernetes, which is normally hard when over 30,000 pods are involved in the time for scheduling are normal reduced, due to control measures taken by the management. In other instances, there is a way in which reduction in speed is catered for by increasing the number of pods within Kubernetes.

Naturally, some of the things you have learned in this process are important to developers and controllers of the designed application. By listing the pods in the first place, some of the informal complications are absorbed in the system or managed by the scheduler control tool. When using the informal, such as the sync, the application is required to be restarted to enable the resources to be assembled in such a way that they perform their intended duties. In this case, the writing controllers are used as the guidance of the watches and the informers of sync, which continue to update regularly. In case it does not work as intended, the developer is required to take another appropriate action; however, the updating of the system activities is not required, meaning there is no need for taking the control measures that would later be rendered useless and a waste of resources.

Chapter Six:
Monitoring Kubernetes

Kubernetes Monitoring Goals

As depicted in the Kubernetes clusters, it is the kubelet that serves as a bridge between the nodes and the master. They run on each node to maintain a set of pods in the kubelet, as it normally manages the activities carried by the pods and code in the application. It is also responsible for collecting statistics for container usage from the Docker's Container Advisor to different components within the system.

The monitoring of Kubernetes nodes requires the application of different methods and approaches, which need to be openly considered. There is the **Daemon Sets pod**, which is inclined to be responsible for the virtual enablement of single deployment on each cluster machine. Unfortunately, the pod is terminated, while the nodes are destroyed. In these cases, the DaemonSet is a structure used by numerous monitoring solutions to allow for the deployment of an agent on every cluster node.

The combination of `Grafana+heapster+InfluxDB` enhances the easy monitoring of the Kubernetes cluster nodes. This combination is otherwise known as the **Kubernetes dashboard**.

Heapster is a basic UI based monitoring goal that is responsible for penetrating your computer data and allows you to see your memory usage and the CPU section on the Kubernetes dashboard. The database is required by the hipster to enhance the collection and storage of data, so they can be retrieved easily when needed. Influxdb allows for the oversimplification of data.

Another monitoring goal is the **Sensu**, which is used independently to monitor Kubernetes. To deploy a sensing agent, the sidecar pattern must be practically applied alongside your container, and the container can be easily maintained by the Kubernetes pods. However, the common monitoring tool of the Kubernetes is **Prometheus**. It is a member of the Cloud Native Computing Foundation, and it's a driving force in the community. It was first developed by SoundCloud and donated afterward to the CNCF, which is Google Borg Monitor motivated. Data is stored as a time series by Prometheus, and it can be retrieved through the Promo query language and visualized with a built-in expression browser. Installation of Prometheus is done directly as a single binary, which can be maintained as a Docker container on your host.

A tracing system delivered by Uber Technologies is **Jaeger**, which serves as a troubleshooter and monitors transactions in systems distributed in a

119

complex way. With the invention of the distribution system and microwaves, distributed context propagation, distributed transaction monitoring, and latency optimization can all be classified under problems. Moreover, the **Weave Scope** is used by Kubernetes to create a map of processes, hosts, and containers in a Kubernetes cluster to help in the real-time understanding of Docker containers. It can be used to run diagnostic commands on containers without excluding the graphical UI. The best graphical tool that can easily assist you to obtain a visual overview of your Kubernetes clusters such as the infrastructure, application, and cluster node connections is the Weave Scope. Monitoring allows you to heal your application when problems are encountered on your road to success.

The **SSE** of Kubernetes will entail proper monitoring of the application to suit the responsibility; therefore, effective monitoring requires effort, forethought, and great tools to enable you to acquire visibility of what is going on in your systems. The following sections will outline some of the reasons why monitoring may be important in the administration of Kubernetes, as well as some more methods for how you can go about monitoring your system:

Exposing metrics and logs will enable you to understand whatever is going on in your system.

Visibility is necessary, though it may not be enough for monitoring. Without proper visibility, monitoring may not be quite possible; therefore, visibility may be just one of the important reasons why monitoring needs to be effectively conducted. The convenient tool that can be efficiently used in from your workstation to identify and manage status is the **Kubectl**. It is the point of beginning and the command line tool for Kubernetes visibility, due to its ability to interact with clusters.

Easy monitoring of your workloads and application is easily enhanced by **Retrace**. This method can be adapted in any environment due to its capability to manage applications. You will acquire all the visibility you require inside your systems, which are deployed inside your Kubernetes when you efficiently apply Retrace to monitor your system.

Being aware of what is happening in the systems you deploy is critical, so monitoring should be the center of the confident operations of your software systems. As monitoring is equally important in deployment models, some unique challenges are presented by Kubernetes clusters resulting from the dynamic nature of resources that come and go. Monitoring goes beyond tools only—it also requires a mindset that can care about the users' wants and needs, and how best they can get technical experience. You will only be ready to create value when you are armed with a desire to develop new tools with and like Kubernetes and allow the installation of great systems in them.

You will need to know when your systems are characterized by continuous break down, which will require remediation. For any organization that takes pleasure in serving their users consistently, monitoring will be their lifeblood. Previously, monitoring was only useful to an operations group with manual effort and rudimentary tools that could watch logs on a single server. That kind of world has vanished, as newly created organizations apply serverless platforms, cloud-native deployments, and container orchestration engines that can cause an explosion of different types of system components, which can all develop into problems. This calls forth great innovative minds and allows users to gain excellent experiences and technical professionalism, thereby giving monitoring more concentration to ensure that these technical skills and knowledge do not get wasted. Monitoring will ensure both developers and their clients stick to the organization's objectives and policies.

With a growing number of clients, technology firms will see tremendous value in leveling the New Relic platform to transition and enable them to manage their application workloads in Kubernetes, thus allowing for the development of new monitoring tools designed for Kubernetes environments. Customers will be constantly on the move of these monitoring capabilities are put into effect. Confidence will be instilled in them when they adopt Kubernetes, allowing them to orchestrate and manage their container workloads.

If, by any chance, the monitoring capabilities are fully put into use, the Kubernetes Application Manager will be able to control application deployments and updates and acquire visibility into working data, like the number of resources used in each cluster and pod namespaces. Effective monitoring of Kubernetes will help identify technical faults and their sources without much effort, thereby allowing for easy creation of solutions to these faults. Auto-discovery of the parts and map relationships between objectives in the cluster-Kubernetes nodes, deployments, namespaces, and replicas will be enabled due to effective monitoring techniques.

Monitoring of Kubernetes will help you ensure that resources allocated to working nodes are sufficient for the deployment of applications and maintaining enough nodes in your cluster. Properly educated decisions will be ensured when several instances—which would also count backup instances—in a node are defined. Healthy conditions of the nodes will also be ensured because of effective monitoring of the CPU and Kubernetes node's memory.

Effective monitoring of Kubernetes will ensure that easy identification of resource limitations is done and all required pods in a deployment are working. Spikes track in resource consumption and understand the frequency of failed container requests on a certain code, the former which is ensured when good monitoring techniques are put to use. Kubernetes-hosted services and applications monitoring solutions are to be provided by the applications manager. They will enable you to effectively manage services to keep your deployed applications running at optimal performance. They will also be mostly engaged in the following activities:

- Close supervision of the outlier's performance of the Kubernetes-hosted applicants operating inside the cluster to help in the identification of individual errors.

- Status view of the node components and Kubernetes master. These node components include the API server, etcd key/value store, controller, and scheduler.

- Regulation of the continuing volume storage consumed by pods and continued volume claim that enables exclusive consumer usage to storage pods.

Alerting capabilities will be brought to you successfully by the applications manager's Kubernetes performance monitoring software. These capabilities are system-level metrics that allow for quick troubleshooting on basic sections of the cluster. Generations of various statistical reports on all significant performances allow for analysis of past trends for making knowledgeable decisions.

To ensure that your applications are healthy and running in the containers created by Kubernetes, some assistance will have to be provided. Specification of probes can be made when you categorize containers that you want to run on your pod. Using **Dashboard** as a web user interface for your Kubernetes cluster will enhance you to allow mutation of your Kubernetes resources that are best left unused. The Dashboard will help you change things; for example, if you wanted to have immutable services and deployments created, updated, and managed by deployment pipelines.

The Kubernetes monitoring tools that are perceptive, like Applications Manager's Kubernetes monitoring software, allow administrators to adapt various Kubernetes cluster monitoring strategies to allow for accountability of the new infrastructure layers introduced during adaptation of containers and the container orchestration, with a distributed Kubernetes working environment. Monitoring of

125

Kubernetes using a sidecar pattern is the most flexible, as it will allow for automatic application of the Kube hosts used for monitoring Kubernetes itself. Kubernetes should not be monitored from Kubernetes, because your monitoring will go down if Kubernetes goes down.

Developing a Monitoring Stack

Creating a platform for monitoring, logging, and alerting is essential for the Kubernetes components in the observable stack. It is important to set up the digital ocean Kubernetes cluster for monitoring to stack all the resources through the debug and have a proper analysis of the application error. These normally consist of house metrics through a series of a metric data visualization layer. Also, the alerting layers are typically used in handling the alerts and integration of the external alerts, which may trigger the application action from outside forces and manage these alerts properly without much difficulty. It is worth noting that the metric data produced is usually visualized and processed within the application for alert notification by the stack.

There are various popular monitoring tools that are usually used by the provider of the application, including the Grafana, Prometheus, and Alert manager stacks. These tools are usually deployed alongside the node-exporter, **Kube-state-metric**, which is the basic cluster of the Kubernetes objects. It involves high-level metric machines like memory usage and the CPU of the computer. Moreover, the Grafana and the Prometheus metrics dashboards are normally redesigned after some time and, through the digital ocean, Kubernetes machines cluster is released for the quick restarting process. On the other hand, the monitoring teams are eager to implement Prometheus-Gafana, which is the monitoring tools. In this case, the alert managers are tasked with manifesting the Prometheus metrics in the application system, and the alert managers cluster help in monitoring the preconfigured alerts which may arise within the Grafana dashboard, which ensures that all the codes are running within the application system. It also helps improve the running of the application and the efficiency it can handle other tasks, within the specification of the application it was designed to perform.

Just like the screen with great components on their visibility, the industry tends to provide application security management on a single platform; therefore, combining the application security into a major driver has become part of the culture of developers, which has evolved over time. The Kubernetes reserve a monitoring dashboard with a prominent display and inbuilt of the stack, which normally keeps an eye on different things within the containers. This involves user interaction in the application and infrastructure usage. For this reason, there are many data-driven decisions that are provided by the users, which normally provide a platform for the services delivery. Moreover, the situation at hand normally involves many perspectives of service delivery, from a simple bug-blocking functionality to other infrastructure issues that may arise in the system application. In this case, the developers try to minimize or avoid the issues that may deter users from accessing their services.

Furthermore, human resources tends to make some of the mistakes that can be avoided and, for this reason, the engineers of the software tend to provide or find the root cause of production issues that may arise, even just once. There are a great many things that could happen, and it is not uncommon—but when the services are monitored well, some of these potential issues can be avoided entirely. Developers and engineers not need to blame each other for things that happen during production or service delivery of the system application; all they need to do is to prevent someone who may cause similar mistakes in the future.

It is prudent to learn from the mistakes and the imperfect decision we normally make by using a variety of tools that can check and monitor the development process of codes during the production.

By doing so, the service providers can always create valid and proper behavior, which ensures a much better outcome. Most of the time, it is good to review the tools that aid in creating a favorite environment for service delivery of Kubernetes. These are enhanced through implementation, and fixing the issues that may invalidate the functionality of the system application.

To facilitate the recovery process, some factors are taken into consideration, which includes diving into the code lifecycle from inception up to serving core customers. For every step, there are different checks that aid to iterate and validate the core factors. It is advisable to fix the bugs while they are still fresh and in their early stages than trying to find them later when they cannot be fixed. To do so, there are some process tools at your disposal.

Foremost, it is worth noting that no code is directly pushed into the master branch, which is the place where the checks start. The pull request opens up immediately and the integrated test and automated units pass through the global average and are reduced to existing codes, which tend to be higher than the normal codes. In case there's a failure in the test, PR will prevent the check from merging, thus creating a warning for the attempt in the Kubernetes application.

In most cases, the PR usually requires approval before the margins, thus creating a low-hanging fruit. These create a functionality of the coverage for high enough teams of mutual reviewing during the production process, which is made through the confidence initially created.

It is common for new errors to arise during the production process, where the new codes are being shipped. During such periods, the provider or developer is prone to receive notifications accompanied by little stack traces, on which the error details are recorded. After receiving all these errors via notification of the system, the provider is able to roll back the code, depending on the previous release, in order to fix the issue. This can go through many circles and, in the end, it must be resolved. There is a direct feedback loop, which involves the time between the development and the time the report is given for fixing directly from the developer.

After the codes have reached the production, it is on to monitor the performance of the infrastructure and security details through the verification of the newly introduced codes. These normally have a negative impact on the key metrics alerts of the application ignored by their users. In case there are memory leaks, security bugs, or performance issues, one can easily debug the application process to its normal use. These are done when the deployment strategies to be used are pinpointed at the beginning or the end when the issues arise.

Therefore, it is advisable to have a small deployment than having larger deployment structures that may occupy a big space for the codes. By doing so, they are reduced the amount of codes needed in the application, thus reducing the problem identification process. For instance, the introduction of other forms of performance issues that normally arise in the system is eliminated through the use of small covers. These small covers make the data more readable and accessible through different angles.

This is all to facilitate the flow migration of a new format in the database, thus meeting the functionality of the Kubernetes. In this case, updates are made properly, whereby the performance slowly deteriorates. There is a time when it is not an acceptable threshold arranged by the codes, and the system would notify the provider of the program about the problem that exists in the system. When that happens, the deployment introduction is facilitated to fix the problem before it gets out of hand. For this reason, there is a need to identify, though the time at which the problem occured and the exact cause of the event are normally difficult to pinpoint.

There are some tools normally used for the deployment and monitoring processes, and these tools need to look into the smallest details to ensure that everything is okay.

- Normally costs are hosted, and GitHub is used for review on the code that is usually built on AWS CodeBuild and Jenkins. The code is generally captured within the Codecov, and the sentry is used for errors, and exceptions are tracked within the software and centralized through the Loggly tool application.

- There is a potential use of the New Relic tool for monitoring different aspects within the application of Kubernetes. The combination of Datadog on CloudWatch also creates a condition for monitoring infrastructure that aids in providing the security needed.

- The application depends on Gmail and the slacks for notification on incidents management.

On the other hand, there is a need to evaluate how the slacks are being managed and the value created by the code in the application. Here, we focused on covering the content and the explanation of the monitoring tools used in the application. There is always a need to understand all these processes and the tools used by the system to create a new and valid monitoring process that will enable the application to function well, as required by the developers. In the case that there are Datadog monitoring tools used by the providers that tend to be suitable for evaluation, chances are high that the mongo cluster may stop responding, thus triggering PagerDuty incidents. There is also the possibility that the master node would go down and the read replica would follow suit.

At one point, the still foggy baby walking in the middle of the night can still get back to the basics of the check-to-buy software error, which arises from the town of the database not responding properly. In this case, the service availability may go down, which is creating PagerDuty incidents that arise from the New Relic monitoring tool.

While at night, the goal of the repair may underline things by increasing memory limit enhancement within the containers, there is the possibility of restoring the accessibility, which can be done through removing unused collections, adding more containers. and restarting machines. This can be done by freeing up the RAM with an aid of increasing the capability of I/O of the application.

Sometimes, it is good to point out or identify the game that is going wrong and identify the ways in which it can be corrected. In this case, swapping is a more of a Datadog infrastructure monitoring tool than it is needed for freeing up the memory. After this has been done by the user's provider, there is a need to restart the culprit machine, which has a problem, and restoring the functionality of the application when the master starting swapping procedure is done. There's also the issue of keeping up with the load, which may be more difficult for the user to manage. All the slack processes are needed to be handled carefully for one not to risk complicating the entire software application.

According to the key findings and analysis of the exploration of the system, the increase in output-input normally triggers retry logic, which can increase the system load. These are normally triggered offline and, when it comes back online, the pressure may be higher with a struggling mongo cluster.

Therefore the user should always seek to understand what is happening and the key incidents that are created in the system's availabilities. The on-call engineers should be kept involved throughout the night as part of the monitoring solution. Riding solo problems are being eliminated and, when they happen, people will always be there to encounter them before they enter the entire system. Through proper monitoring, some of the problems can be eliminated or done away with without much struggle.

Naturally, it is not good to wake somebody up in the middle of the night to provide an appropriate service, and there are setup times for people to sleep with no disturbances expected. Remember that system failure is also due to some of the complications caused by the tiredness in the application.

What to Monitor

In this next part, we will be concerned with what we have to monitor in the Kubernetes application system, and the main focus will be on how these tools are monitored and structured toward their functionality. The Kubernetes architectures create a firm foundation on how the application is built to carry out various activities that need to be critically monitored in the system. We dig deeper into these values, which make the whole structure functional and effective for the users, providers of the application, and general outlook of the Kubernetes monitoring system.

The application monitoring always engages two questions: why is this happening, and what is happening? The machine used to address the data questions, which normally involves the remedy of the action. They usually come in different forms, as in, metrics and logs. The issue addressed, in this case, is more crucial and fundamental to the users, and the providers who wish to use the application in the future make it work easier for everyone.

The time series always makes the metrics measure what is happening in the workload of the system

135

application. It tends to gauge the current consumption metrics, which are used in various engines. Moreover, the problems have to be solved using different metrics for measuring the problems, which may occur in the application. The current state of behaviors is handled in such a way that every warning sign is handled as urgent.

By monitoring the logs, one is able to know when things happen in the application system, and it usually provides records of events that have occurred most often in the system. The tool contains much information, and it provides a clear context of the action taken by the Kubernetes, securing the errors that are breaking in the application.

Kubernetes usually has a comprehensive setup of machine data, which is linked to the application to answer and monitor the inquiries of the users. It is run inside the Kubernetes data clusters, where it collects all the information needed by the provider. By doing so, it's normally using common metrics that help the tools in monitoring what is going on in the Kubernetes. This data is normally written in GoLang, where essential metrics are revealed in the runtime. This matrix is usually necessary for the GoLang processes, which are bound within the application system; however, the common metrics are related to the etcd found within the node tool. Here is where multiple components interact with the etcd, and it's a major reason for keeping an eye on the issues that may arise. Therefore, it is necessary to analyze the GoLang metrics and stats of the common etcd metrics within the Kubernetes components.

We would also monitor the cabinet control plane, whereby the engine that powers the Kubernetes components is critically analyzed. According to the observation, multiple parts of the containerized application are grouped together to work as a common unit. In this case, each piece has a specific function that must be monitored to validate the health state of the component. These are normally done through the control plane of the Kubernetes. One should note that every component of the application is critical to its function within the system.

Furthermore, we have to monitor the API server, which provides the front-end and the central point of the Kubernetes cluster. It is responsible for all the interaction within the components of the API server, which is also the central function units of the Kubernetes. The fundamental role of this component is the **apserver_request account**, which dispenses the HTTP response content and the type code used in the system. It is also responsible for the quarter request latencies.

Monitoring the etcd of the Kubernetes application system is important, as it provides key value stores for all the application's information. These must be monitored to ensure that all the data within the system are as per the set requirement of the provider or the developer to the users. The data integrated into these components represents the key state of the Kubernetes cluster and how they carry out the basic activities where they reside. In this case, some of the metrics are used to measure the impact of the data within the components of the Kubernetes. One needs to monitor the etcd server leader to ensure if the 1 leader truly exists, and a 0 if it does not exist. There is also a need to detect any change in the leader that may exist when the application is altered or run in the system. The proposal applied in the etcd server is accounted for in Kubernetes, and the total is committed in the monitoring server, which ensures that they are appropriately analyzed and within the specified number needed in the application.

Here, the number of etcd server proposals pending and fails are scrutinized by the developer to come up with the right criteria for selecting the best ones to be used within the Kubernetes. Some of the metrics that measure the etcd debugging of the MVCC can be integrated into the system to gauge the total size of the bytes used by the Kubernetes application when it is run in its cluster. It monitors the size of the database used and the history compaction of the application data. The latency distribution that the etcd commits is also accounted for in the backend nature.

Ultimately, the scheduler of the Kubernetes is monitored in order to watch the newly created pods in the Kubernetes. The aim is to determine the way in which the nodes are able to run the pods within the application. The decision is normally made based on the data already within the system, which serves as the source requirement of the pods. In this case, the scheduling latency is monitored to establish the visibility of any delays, which may hinder the scheduler from its functionality. End-to-end scheduling latency is monitored to establish the scheduling algorithm, which binds the latency of the application within microseconds.

Final Words

Software developers can attest that containers have offered flexibility to run cloud native applications on virtual and physical infrastructure. Containers package the services comprising of applications makes them portable across varying computer environments for use in development, testing, and production. For instance, it is possible to ramp application instances to match spikes quickly with containers. Because containers draw resources from the host OS, they tend to be much lighter in weight compared to VMs. This means that, containers make utmost use of the underlying server infrastructure.

Being an open source system for scaling, managing, and deploying containerized applications, Kubernetes handles scheduling container tasks onto computer clusters and further manages the arising workloads with the aim of ensuring they operate as the user envisioned. This all further means that, Kubernetes combines software development and operations through design, as opposed to bolting on operations as an afterthought. In addition, Kubernetes supports the order of magnitude increase, in regards to operations of modern software systems through the use of declarative and infrastructure agnostic constructs that describe how applications interact, how they are managed, as well as how they are created.

Developers are called upon to develop applications that can operate across multiple operating environments like virtualized private clouds, dedicated on-prem servers, as well as public clouds like Azure and AWS. Before, applications and their supporting tooling were closely tied to underlying infrastructure; this made it costly to apply other applicable deployment models, despite the advantages they offered. Applications were highly dependent on specific environments, as per different respects such as: performance issues that were associated to pre-determined network architecture and adherence to specific constructs based on cloud providers. Note that PaaS tries to resolve such issues, but there is a caveat: strict requirements are imposed in areas like application frameworks and programming languages. As such, PaaS is not preferred by many development teams. Through offering core container capabilities without imposing various restrictions, Kubernetes does away with the infrastructure lock-in, which is achieved through a combination of features such as services and pods within the Kubernetes platform.

Evidently, from the information in this book, Kubernetes creates a breakthrough for DevOps by allowing teams to keep up with the modern software development requirements. When Kubernetes is absent, teams are forced to script their unique software deployment, update, and scale workflows. This explains why some organizations prefer to hire large IT teams who can handle such tasks alone. Kubernetes is designed to ensure that users derive maximum utility from applicable containers, enabling them to build cloud native applications that can run independently and anywhere. This makes Kubernetes an effective and efficient application development and operation model that has been missing on many application teams.

Kubernetes is not a traditional PaaS system because it operates at the container level, as opposed to the hardware level. Instead, it offers some applicable features that are common to what PaaS offers, such as: load balancing monitoring, logging, and deployment. It is important to note that such default settings are pluggable and optional, since Kubernetes is not monolithic. What is important is that Kubernetes offers the ideal building blocks for creating developer platforms while preserving flexibility and user choices where necessary. It is also important to note that Kubernetes is not just a mere orchestration system; it eliminates the need for orchestration. This is because it contains a set of independent and composable control processes, triggering the system to support the desired state.

Kubernetes has a lot to offer, especially to data scientists who are interested in the development of techniques that can solve critical business challenges through machine learning. Most importantly, it offers the end users more advantages because machine learning represents varying workloads that can train models and offer insights. Machine learning is applied in a production as a crucial part of an intelligent application.

www.ingramcontent.com/pod-product-compliance
Lightning Source LLC
LaVergne TN
LVHW050142060326
832904LV00004B/122